Norway South

Bernhard Pollmann

Norway South

50 selected valley and mountain walks
between Oslo, Lom, Bergen and Kristiansand

With 69 colour photos, 50 walking maps
and an overview map

ROTHER · MUNICH

Front cover:
From Nosi, on the western edge of the Hardangervidda,
the view spans across the Søfjord and beyond to the glacier-covered
Folgefonn peninsula.

Frontispiece (photo on page 2):
Houses along the southern coast near Mandal (Photo: M. Waeber).

All photos were taken by Bernhard Pollmann, except for
pp. 2, 25, 33, 85, 87, 91, 128, 150, 151 Michael Waeber,
and pp. 24, 27, 74, 78 Peter Mertz.

Cartography:
Waking maps and overview map © Bergverlag Rother Munich
(drawn by cartographer Christian Rolle, Holzkirchen)

Translation: C. Ade Team (Andrea Adelung)

1st edition 2001
© Bergverlag Rother GmbH, Munich
ISBN 3-7633-4807-7

Distributed in Great Britain by Cordee, 3a De Montfort Street, Leicester
Great Britain LE1 7HD, www.cordee.co.uk
in USA by AlpenBooks, 3616 South Road, C-1, Mukilteo,
WA 98275 USA, www.alpenbooks.com

ROTHER WALKING GUIDES

Crete West · Iceland · Mallorca · Mont Blanc · Norway South · Provence · Sardinia · Valais East ·
Around the Zugspitze

**Dear mountain lovers! We would be happy to hear your opinion and
suggestions for amendment to this Rother walking guide.**

Bergverlag Rother · Munich
D-85521 Ottobrunn · Haidgraben 3 · Tel. (089) 608669-0 · Fax -69
Internet www.rother.de · E-mail bergverlag@rother.de

Preface

In 50 walks, this guide opens up Southern Norway between Oslo, Lom, Bergen and Kristiansand: its range spans from the highest peaks of Northern Europe in the Jotunheimen National Park, to the picturesque forests and lakes in Telemark and the high heathland areas over the waterfall-rich Setesdal valley, from the cliff scenery in Rogaland and on the glacier-covered Folgefonn peninsula, to the panoramic domes and plant oases of Rondane National Park, from the mountains near Oslo, to Hårteigen, the Sphinx of the Hardangervidda – in a setting which leaves no wishes unfulfilled regarding variety and beauty of the countryside.

Introducing a selection of walks for every physical condition, this guide describes »easy« and »difficult« routes – family-friendly walks are included, as well as climbs up exposed peaks, challenging day-long walks, and tours covering several days from hut to hut. Furthermore, alternative routes are presented, including walks up to the starting site of glacier tours. Since Southern Norway occupies an area approximately the size of the whole of Southern Germany, the 50 route descriptions are preceded by an information section, as well as a short description of all mountain areas.

Whether you select an easy or difficult tour, covering a few hours or several days: Walking in the mountains of the midnight sun requires prudence and constant concentration; yet this is exactly what makes up a great part of the fascination of being underway in the fjell – to have all senses challenged, to experience oneself as part of nature in all its pristine glory, and to act in harmony with it.

Spring 2000   Bernhard Pollmann

Contents

Walking in Norway

Fjell

The mountainous country through which almost all walks in this guide pass is known in Norway as »fjell«: The fjell begins independently of the altitude of the upper coniferous tree line, and includes that part of the mountain range which, at least in previous centuries, remained untouched by economic utilisation and permanent human settlement. The word »fjell« is related to the German word »Feld«, English »field«, and originally referred to the spacious mountain plateaux formed by glaciers of the Ice Age, which are so characteristic of Scandinavia.

Today, »fjell« refers to all mountainous country above the coniferous tree line, whether it is broad and plateau-like or alpine craggy. Thus, with the exception of coniferous forests, fjell walks offer everything that makes a mountain walk a fascinating adventure: peaks and ridges of all levels of difficulty, glaciers, fertile mountain pasture valleys and picturesque lakes, gentle hilltops and steep scree flanks, birch woods and moors, gorges and canyons, thunderous waterfalls – all independent of the elevation above sea level. The elevation of the coniferous tree line varies greatly in Norway: In Østlandet, in eastern Norway, it lies at 900–1100m, in Vestlandet, in western Norway, it is only 400–500m, while it sinks to sea level in northern Norway.

Vegetation zones: The fjell above the coniferous tree line is divided into three zones. The most species-rich, but the most uncomfortable to walk, is the »Willow Belt« (vierbeltet); it is characterised by willow species and undergrowth (Lapland, bluegreen, woolly willow, etc.), of fjell birch woods measuring up to 12m and cold-resistant broad-leaved trees such as aspen and mountain ash, as well as generally lush flora, from moorland and heathland and their typical inhabitants, such as Norwegian raspberries, cotton grass, dwarf birch and blueberries.

The Willow Belt, which expanded greatly in the 20th century, reaches elevations of up to 1500m in Jotunheimen. In the vegetation zone above the Willow Belt, grasses and grass-type plants are dominant. This panorama-rich zone can be considered the most comfortable to walk; even mosquitoes, the »plague of the North« (they primarily appear during and after the melting of the snow), are more likely to be found in the Willow Belt. Where the continuous plant cover ends and cliffs, weathered rock, mosses and lichen dominate, lies the High Mountain Belt (høyfjellsbeltet).

Demands – Friliftsliv

In contrast to the comfortable routes in the German low-mountain regions, the routes in Norway's fjell are »difficult«, since they almost always run along paths and inclines: rocky, steep, full of roots and moorland, they lead cross-country, often through scree and boulders; movement is often coupled

A diverse landscape of fjord and fjell awaits the hiker in Rogaland.

with light climbing; interrupted patches along the path at dizzying heights are, with very few exceptions, not secured by railings; depending on the weather, streams can swell considerably and must be waded through.

The concept upon which this type of hiking is based is totally different from that of the German authoritarian state: while in Germany, where powerful bureaucracies and lobbies, through the erection of iron clamps, railings and stairs, or through blasting cliffsides, carving steps and roadways, provide protection from legal recourse from injured parties and allow even inexperienced hikers to access mountains without the necessary familiarisation and respect for nature, hiking in Norway places the emphasis on experiencing unspoilt nature – with all the dangers that unspoilt nature poses to humans. Most of the approximately 4.6 million Norwegians learn to get around in the fjell from an early age, and can handle these dangers.

The basic demands: knowledge of nature, independence, self-responsibility, prudence and intuitive reaction skills, as well as sure footing, good physical condition and a good sense of orientation. With all of these, and the proper equipment, walking in the fjell countryside of the north, hardly touched by civilisation, can be experienced as archaic, relaxing, whimsical, and free. In Norway, this type of being underway is not called »walking«, but rather »Friliftsliv«: »free-air living« – holistic outdoor living in harmony with heaven and earth.

Tents May be pitched anywhere in the uncultivated Utmark (»uncultivated land«).

Allemannsretten – Outdoor camping

The legal framework for »Friluftsliv« is provided by the Allemannsretten (General Law). This law differentiates between the cultivated Innmark (cultivated land) and the uncultivated Utmark (uncultivated land), and permits anyone to move freely throughout the Utmark year-round, as long as this is done in a respectful manner and the respective owner (which can also be the State) has not posted a sign prohibiting it. That means, e.g., that not only can anyone walk in the fjell, but tents May also be pitched freely there. Only in the Innmark area (e.g. near farms; usually fenced in) is this prohibited.

Season

The main cross-country ski season is during Easter holidays. The mid-summer's night, which in the valleys is celebrated as a lively festival, marks the start of the walking season: school and factory holidays are from the end of June / beginning of July to mid-August. Depending on the weather, a great deal of residual snow May be found well into July in elevations from 1000m, and when the snow is melting, walking is very dangerous if not impossible there. The late summer post-season starting in mid-August is recommended: The least amount of precipitation falls, the huts are no longer over-booked, and, along with the residual snow, the mosquitoes have also disappeared. The most picturesque time is the light-intensive, colourful month of September, when, however, temperatures often sink below 0°C at night, and it May snow.

Tourist Information

Use of the Guide

Each route description is prefaced by an overview of the most important information regarding each walk. The *walking time* needed for persons with average physical condition deviates somewhat from the information found in Norwegian maps and guides; these times have, in most cases, been slightly corrected upward. The metres of altitude for the *ascent* are rounded up to the nearest 50 (e.g. 600 instead of 578 metres high). Assume that, as a rule, for every ascent there is a descent of equal height. The accommodation possibilities along the route are listed under *Huts*; see p. 16. In the DNT Office, as well as in most staffed huts, you can obtain a »nøkkel« (key) if you leave a deposit; you do not have to return the nøkkel to the same place in which you received it. In order to be better able to judge tour demands, the tour suggestions (tour numbers) have been highlighted in various colours. They can be interpreted as follows:

BLUE

These walks are usually short, follow marked paths including few inclines of a maximum of 400 metres of altitude in forest, meadow and/or scree and rocky terrain, have no exposed spots, but require sure-footedness. The paths May lead through terrain which is partly boggy grassland with water holes, and May contain passages so small that, in wet weather, the proper protective clothing is required for passing bushes, and general caution is needed because of slippery roots or wet patches of lichen on rocks. Although there May be a sign on the route, for instance, which designates walk 6 as »especially suitable for children and senior citizens«, sure-footedness, sturdy boots and a map are nevertheless necessary. Rock and scree walk 39 and primeval forest walk 40 are also categorised as BLUE: Do not wear sneakers on BLUE routes, but rather, sturdy shoes with good soles.

RED

Certain passages or portions of these routes lead through terrain in which the path is exposed, May require the aid of the hiker's hands, and include steep ascents and descents of a total of up to 800 meters of altitude. In addition to sure-footedness, which is also vital for BLUE routes, RED routes also require the hiker to be vertigo-free and in good condition. Since certain patches of the paths are exposed and May pose a problem, all routes containing even only one exposed »crux« are designated as RED.

For instance, due to exposed passages, walk 3 is categorised as RED; although, with its 400 metres of altitude for the ascent, it only poses minimal demands to physical condition, and primarily runs through simple, BLUE terrain.

BLACK

These routes lead along ascents and descents of over 800 metres of altitude through rocky terrain which can be steep and have passages or spots where the trail is exposed and for which the use of a hand as a hold is necessary. The BLACK routes require sure-footedness, strong physical condition (in the case of longer tours, including the ability to wear a heavy rucksack), the absence of vertigo, orientation skills, knowledge of the weather, and nordic or alpine mountain experience.

Access to Starting Points

Very few starting points for walks described in this guide can be accessed with public transport such as train, bus or boat, but must be reached with a car or taxi. For one-way routes, it is customary to phone a taxi with a mobile phone (ask for the number of the respective taxi company at the starting point or in staffed huts along the route), as soon as you can predict when you will reach the destination of the route.

Often, the starting points are situated at the end of private toll roads, which are usually not well tended (full of potholes, they are often unpaved mountain pasture roads), and can be steep or narrow in stretches. The parking areas at the end of such toll roads are, to some extent, surprisingly large and at times even supervised (if they are near holiday cabin settlements) and/or charge a fee. On the other hand, however, some are only parking bays and are completely isolated.

In general, one has to get used to the fact that many starting points can only be found after a careful search: There are usually no signs, but if you look closely, you will find a *red T* marker and a cairn, and then the path.

By checking the map, you can identify that this is where the route begins; driving directions to such starting points are correspondingly precisely detailed.

We have never had problems with cars being broken into. The fact that a few parking areas and holiday cabin settlements are supervised by professional security services highlights the fact, however, that in Norway, too, the potential for crime is on the rise.

Fishing

In order to be able to fish while on a walk, you first need a national permit, which can be purchased for a low annual fee at the post office, and secondly, a local fishing license, which can also be obtained for a fee at campgrounds, in shops, hotels, etc.

The local fishing license is only valid for a particular area; if you walk into another area, you also need a local fishing license for that area. Only ocean fishing is free of charge – which is why many do so to shorten the wait for the ferry at a fjord.

Information

Tourist information materials can be obtained from the:

Norwegian Tourist Board, 5th Floor, Charles House, 5 Regent Street (Lower), SW1Y 4LR London, ☎ +44 207 839 625, Fax: +44 207 839 601, E-mail: greatbritain@ntr.no

Norwegian Tourist Board, 655 Third Avenue, Suite 1810, New York 1 US-New York, ☎ +1 212 885 9700, Fax: +1 212 885 9710, E-mail: usa@ntr.no

Internet addresses:

http://www.visitnorway.com

http://www.nsbr.no

http://www.skandinavien.de/norwegen

http://www.turistforeningen.no

http://www.fjordnorway.no

Equipment

Equipment containing the following basic elements is recommended for walking in Norway:

- Rucksack: for walks with accommodation in huts, the rucksack must fit a sleeping bag and mat.
- Sun protection: lotion, head covering, lip balm
- Protection against the cold: It is better to have two articles of clothing too many in your rucksack than one too few.
- Protection against the wind
- Protection against moisture: gaiters, backpack rain covering, etc. In rainy weather, we recommend bringing along a change of head covering and socks.
- Mosquito protection: insect oil or stick, etc., preferably purchased in Norway. The primary mosquito season is during and after the snow-melting period.
- Map: a necessary article in the fjell
- Compass: as is the case with a map, a required article
- Altimeter: a good altimeter is a helpful orientation aid in the fjell; it also serves as a barometer.
- Drinking flask and cup
- Provisions: You should always take some food along with you – even if you think your walk will be short.
- Emergency set: Emergency medicines, rescue blanket, whistle, high-power mobile phone with stored emergency numbers, including 113.

Regarding these and other pieces of equipment, we recommend purchasing them only at competent outfitters and not in shops more geared toward fashionable leisure-time themes than safety and functionality in the mountains.

In moorlands, slat or board gangplanks are occasionally available for easier walking. They can be dangerously slippery when wet.

Car traffic

In Norway, driving with dipped headlights is also required during the day. The maximum speed limit outside of built-up areas is 80 kph, and inside built-up areas 50 kph. The legal blood alcohol limit is 0.5 parts per thousand. Violation of these limits can mean harsh punishments. Information on road-blocks can be obtained around the clock from the traffic patrol at ℂ 22 65 40 40.

■ Breakdown service: Members of automobile clubs belonging to the Alliance International du Tourisme (AIT) can receive support in Norway from Norges Automobilforbund (NAF), N-0105 Oslo, ℂ 22 34 14 00, emergency call service ℂ 22 34 16 00, fax 22 42 88 30.

■ Toll roads: Access to several starting points is via toll roads. The toll is approximately 30–50 NKr and must be paid independently at the Bom-stasjon (it will be checked). If you use toll roads often, you should have a supply of 10-krone coins in the car. The toll roads are generally not well kept (wood removal roads, field roads, potholes) and only allow slow driving.

Mountaineering boots

For walks in southern Norway, sturdy hiking or mountaineering boots with non-slip soles and ankle coverage are generally recommended. They are required for fatigue-free walking, slip protection on dry rock, relative safety in marshy terrain, and to prevent ankle injuries. Protection from moisture in grassy terrain and in brush is provided by *gaiters* reaching to under the knee; the zippers on the gaiters should have a protective cover strip, since water can otherwise seep in through the zipper.

In order to reduce the danger of injury while wading through creeks, we additionally recommend taking along *hiking sandals* on walks lasting more than one day.

As an alternative to mountaineering or hiking boots, *natural-rubber boots* (»Gummistøvler«), with treaded soles and steel reinforcement are used in Norway (e.g. for walks in largely boggy terrain). Gummistøvler have the advantage that you can comfortably wade through a creek or river in them, whereas mountaineering boots must be removed and hung around your neck. – In wet weather, it can be advantageous to have a second, dry pair of mountaineering boots in the car.

DNT – Den Norske Turistforening

The Norwegian Mountain Walking Association, DNT, is responsible for the walking infrastructure, including the huts, organising guided walks and offering glacier and climbing courses, among others. Full members (including foreign members) receive the route book »Til fots i fjellet« as well as the DNT newspaper »Fjell og Vidde«, and can use all Hytter at a reduced price. Membership is worth it, financially, if several stays in huts are planned. Membership can be obtained – for one year each – at the address below, as well as in staffed Hytter:

Den Norske Turistforening, Postboks 7 Sentrum (Storgata 3), N-0101 Oslo, ✆ 22 82 28 00, fax 22 82 28 01, Internet http://www.turistforeningen.no/

Shopping – Refreshment Opportunities

Whether you are looking for food or outdoor equipment: As a wealthy, high-tech country, Norway offers a comprehensive range of goods and a dense network of shops and supermarkets. The relatively high prices of a few products, are offset by relatively low prices for other goods (potatoes, baked goods) and services (ferry crossings in fjords).

Shop opening times are regulated in such a varied way that no general statements can be made about them.

Resting options that are conventional e.g. in the alps (mountain guest houses, excursion restaurants) are all but non-existent for walking in the fjell; it is an undisputed fjell rule to have food in your rucksack; besides, there is something cosy about a self-made fire, above which water for coffee or tea is bubbling.

Exclusively depending on the supply of self-serviced huts stocked with provisions is expensive, and not necessarily tasty. On the other hand, the calorie-rich meals in the staffed cabins with meal service are often tasty, indeed; however, you have to arrive at dinner punctually, otherwise there will be nothing left.

If you stay in a staffed hut with food service, your thermos flask (we recommend an unbreakable one) will be filled the following morning with coffee or tea, as desired, for that walking day.

Money

Payment is made in Norwegian currency or with credit cards; electronic cash and electronic wallets are very prevalent.

Eurocheques, still accepted just a few years ago, can no longer be used for payment or to exchange money.

Currently, the simplest and most inexpensive way to get cash is with your Eurocheque bank card: Just about every bank has an automated teller machine, from which you can withdraw money after inserting your bank card, entering your PIN number, and indicating the amount desired. Due to our fast-moving times, however, it is recommended that you find out what the current practises are before you leave for your trip.

Thunder Storms

Assuming you have sure-footedness, no vertigo, a good sense of orientation, and a minimum of climbing skills (e.g. the three-point hold), there is only one other danger when walking in Norway: the weather. Thunder storms occur most frequently in July (less frequently in June and August, hardly ever in May and September). If you can see by the cloud formation that a thunder storm is looming, break off your walk.

Hytter (Huts for overnight accommodation)

For walks in the fjell in Norway, there are three categories of »Hytter« of the DNT or regional hiking associations from which to choose:

■ Staffed huts (betjente hytter) with food service are also accessible to non-members. The standard spans from mountain and sports hotels to secluded mountain guest houses not accessible via public transport. Accommodation is less expensive for DNT members than non-members (approximately 30%). You should plan on a pro capita price of the equivalent of approximately £ 31 ($ 48) per night including meals.

For example, in 1999, it cost 80 NKr (non-members: 155 NKr) for a night's stay in a dormitory at the Fannaråkhytta (sleeping on your own mat with a sleeping bag on the floor cost 50 NKr); dinner, breakfast and a thermos filling cost 223 (300) NKr, for a total of 303 NKr or approximately £ 23.50 ($ 35) for a DNT member. Methods of payment accepted were cash and all standard credit cards. ▮

- Self-serviced huts (selvbetjeningshytter) are locked with a standard DNT lock or are open as long as they are supervised in the summer. In the area of the Stavanger Turistforening (ST), the huts are open. Only members of the DNT or affiliated sub-organisations can obtain the universal key (nøkkel) for the locked cabins – upon leaving a deposit – at the DNT office in Oslo and in the staffed huts. The self-serviced huts are stocked with provisions (expensive). The »self service« is based on the principle of honesty: Costs for accommodation and food taken are placed by the hiker into the cabin cash box. Included in the »self service« principle are clean-up tasks such as washing dishes, sweeping, and perhaps chopping wood. ◪

- Unstaffed huts (unbetjente hytter) differ from self-serviced cabins in that they are not stocked with provisions; hikers must bring their own food. ⌂

During summer holidays and at Easter, you can assume that the huts will be operating at capacity: Thus, it is advisable to take along a mat and sleeping bag. In the off-season, taking along a sleeping bag is usually sufficient – unless a class of schoolchildren has filled the hut. Many huts tend to be over-filled during hunting season as well. All DNT members have the right to sleep in a hut, even if it is over-filled . . .

The DNT Mountain Hotel Haukeliseter.

Maps

Among the ground rules for walking in the fjell is taking along hiking maps. The coloured map sketches in this guide which accompany every recommended walk and indicate the course of the route are an important component of each hike recommendation. In addition, this guide cites hiking maps published in various scales based on national topographical maps (Turkart, indicated in this guide as TurK) and / or topographical maps on a scale of 1:50,000 (indicated here as TK 50). We recommend using not only the topographical maps, but also the tour maps, since they are often more up-to-date than the topographical maps (some of which are decades old, even if they are purchased as part of the »new« red series). If you wish to orient yourself on a more widespread level, it is a good idea to also bring along a road map. The best road maps, from a hiking perspective, are Cappelens Bil- og Turistkart on a scale of 1:325,000; they show the main hiking routes (with time indications) and the hiking cabins. The road maps of Southern Norway and Central Norway, published by freytag&berndt, (each 1:400,000), also show hiking routes.

Medical Care

Comprehensive medical care is of high quality in Norway, which, among other things, is due to the fact that patients must pay for a portion of their treatment themselves (in the case of dental work, patients pay for all of their treatment). The respective local »Legevakt«, to where you can go, is signposted on the streets, and hospitals are indicated as »sykehus«.

Pharmacies

There is no medication which you can get in Norwegian pharmacies (apotek) without a prescription; this even applies to aspirin. If you need medication, you should bring it with you from your home country.

Emergency calls

The following universal emergency telephone numbers are valid throughout Norway: Fire brigade 110, police 112, ambulance 113.

Languages

Most Norwegians speak English well. Norway's independence from Denmark in 1814 led to the development of two official languages: Bokmål (book language), a language influenced by Danish, and Nynorsk (New Norwegian), a »people's language«, which began developing in the 19th Century from Norwegian dialects. In 1877, »New Norwegian« Nyorsk was granted the same legal status as the national language, thus making Norway officially bilingual. The development of a uniform language for the whole of Norway (Samnorsk) has not been achieved to date; thus, Norway still has two

In the fjell, the greeting is usually »Heil« (singular) or »Hei Heil« (plural). The accent is almost always on the first syllable (Róndane, Jótuneimen, Mémurubu, etc.). For the Norwegian u in English, say a long »e« while pursing your lips in an »o« position; Norwegian »du« is informal for »you«. The Norwegian å is similar to a long »o« in English, and for the Norwegian ø in English, say a long »a« while pursing your lips in an »o« position.

å, åa	= (small) river	ledig	= unoccupied
åpen	= open	myr, -a	= bog, swamp
bekk, -en	= stream, brook	nasjonalpark	= national park
bratt	= steep	nøkkel	= key
bre, -en	= glacier	nord	= north, northerly
bro, -a/bru, -a	= bridge	øst	= east, easterly
botn, botnen	= inner end of a valley or fjord	råken	= ridge
		ras, -et	= avalanche
bu, -a	= (mountain pasture)cabin	regn, -et	= rain
by, byen	= town	regnbyger	= rain shower
dal, -en	= valley	røde T	= red T
døla	= river flowing through a valley	seter/sæter, setra	= mountain pasture
egg, -en	= ridge	skard, -er	= wind gap, col
elv, -a	= river	skog, -en	= forest
fare, -n	= danger	sjø, sjøen	= lake, sea
farlig	= dangerous	snø, -en	= snow
fjell, -et	= mountainous country above the coniferous tree line	sol, -a	= sun
		sør	= south, southerly
fly, -a	= plateau	stengt	= closed
fonn, -a	= firn	sti, -en	= path, mountain path
forbudt	= prohibited	støl, -en	= mountain pasture (-cabin)
foss, -en	= waterfall	telt, -et	= tent
full, fult	= full, no vacancy	Telting forbudt	= camping prohibited
fylke	= province	tind, -en	= summit (alpine)
gjuv, -et	= gorge	tjøm, tyørnet	= lake
gjel, -et	= deep and narrow gorge	topp, -en	= peak (general)
haug, -en	= hill	ur, -a	= scree
hei, -a	= heath	utsikt, -en	= view
hø, -a	= hilltop	vær, været	= weather
høgd, -a	= height, rise, mountain range	varde, -n	= stone figure, - marker
		vatn, et,	
hol, holet	= cirque valley	vannet	= lake
hytte, hytta	= hut, mountain hotel	vei, -en	= street, accessible road
is, -en	= ice	vest	= west, westerly
juv, -et	= gorge	vidde, vidda	= plateau

Abbreviations

m. alt.	= metres of altitude		on a scale of 1:50,000
TK 50	= topographical map	TurK 100	= Turkart 1:100,000

names: In Nynorsk, Norway is called »Noreg« in Bokmål it is »Norge«. For tourists to Norway, this means that they will be confronted with two different versions on signs, maps, etc. This guide, including the map excerpts, exclusively uses the »high language« (Bokmål); thus, a few town names deviate from the topographical map.

Road conditions / Fuelling

The Norwegian public network of roads – in contrast to the private toll roads – are of standard quality and can be compared to German roads. The term »Riksvei« (national road), in combination with a number, indicates streets which are comparable to A roads in the UK. The narrow width of some mountain roads do not allow for two lanes; signs with the letter M (Møteplass = »meeting place«) indicate wide areas in which one can wait and allow oncoming traffic to pass. Petrol stations (petrol is more expensive than in Germany and Denmark; diesel is the most inexpensive) are widespread, however not all will accept bank cards or credit cards.

Snow: Assume that toll roads in higher elevations can be covered with snow (and not ploughed), even after the calendar begin of summer. Count on mountain roads having snowfall from September on, and drive with snow tyres (in Norway, spikes are used in snow or when snow is expected to fall), and, to be on the safe side, take snow chains along with you. Most road maps indicate which mountain pass roads are ploughed on a year-round basis.

Telephoning

To phone from Norway to the USA: 001 plus the area code and number. The country code for the UK is 0044. To call Norway from other countries: dial the country code 0047 first.

Accommodation on your trip

Hotel prices in Norway are relatively high; the exquisite breakfast buffets in the hotels, on the other hand, are relatively inexpensive, and all are accessible for a breakfast fee (even to non-guests, including hikers in walking attire).

A relatively inexpensive alternative to accommodation in a hotel are the »Hytter« (huts, chalets), indicated as such on street signs, found on camping grounds and farms. The hytter have varying furnishings, sizes and prices. They are so popular in season that it is almost impossible to find ones with vacancy (»ledig«), especially on weekends (»fult« = full). Bring your own provisions when staying in the hytter.

If you like sleeping in a tent, you will enjoy the hytter, because, among other reasons, they offer better noise protection, which can certainly be an advantage on some campgrounds.

Entry into Norway

Norway is not an EU nation. You must present a passport or personal identification card upon entry. Drivers of motor vehicles also require a license and the automobile registration documents. Import regulations are so complex that you should have the current list sent to you by the Norwegian Tourist Office if you are planning to bring along more than just »normal« travel items.

»Constructed« hiking paths are rare in the fjell, such as the »Munketreppene« (Monks' Steps), which are said to have been built by medieval monks.

Mountain Areas and Landscapes

Blefjell (walk 44 and 48)

The Blefjell is a 19-km long quartzite ridge in Telemark, which rises far above the surrounding low mountains between Numedal Valley and Tinnsjø Lake. At its highest elevation, the Bletoppen (1342m), it offers an excellent summit view. The coniferous forest in the Blefjell climbs over the 1000-m mark in places and often forms the forest boundary instead of birch trees.

Breheimen (walk 25)

Breheimen (Glacier home) is the western Norwegian high-mountain and glacier countryside between the Jotunheimen and the interior foothills of Sognefjord and Nordfjord. The core is the plateau glacier **Jostedalsbreen**, which, with its 480 km^2, is the largest glacier in continental Europe. Since 1991, it and its surroundings have been under protection as a national park (1230km^2).

From the interior foothills of the Sognefjord in the south, the Jostedalsbreen stretches about 100km to the north-east, its width reaching up to 15km. This tremendous mass of ice, measuring up to 500m, reaches an elevation of 1700–1900m above sea level on the surface, and peaks at Høgste Breakulen (approximately 1957m). Only very few rocks show through the mass of ice, among them the highest, the Lodalskåpa (2083m).

The Jostedalsbreen extends over 50 glacial arms and waterfalls in all directions, a few of which are important tourist attractions, such as the **Brigsdalsbreen** in Stryn on the west side, and the **Nigardsbreen** in Luster on the east side. All Breheimen glaciers together cover an area of over 800km^2. The combination of fjord and fjell, ice and fertile mountain pasture valleys make Breheimen a diverse countryside rich with unique beauty.

The Jostedalsbreen is named after the legendary **Jostedalen**, which slices deeply through the mountains of Breheimen on the east side of the glacier. The 50-km long valley is accessible via the Riksvei 604, and is considered one of the most significant tourist attractions of the country.

The **Breheimsenteret**, accessible from the Jostedalen valley, in the foreground of the Nigardsbreen, is a glacier, national park, nature, sports, and cultural history museum (N-5827 Jostedal, ✆ 57 68 32 50, Internet http://www.jostedal.com).

In season, daily glacier tours of the Jostedalsbreen Breførarlag on the Nigardsbreen start at Breheimsenteret; Jostedalsbreen Breførarlag also offers glacier courses (N-5827 Jostedal, ✆ 57 68 31 11, Internet http://www.home.sol.no/~josbre).

The Skåla rises in the west and not the south of Norway, but it is nevertheless introduced to represent the Jostedalsbreen glacier tours, and as an appetiser for walks in the marvellous countryside of the west Norwegian fjordlands.

Impressive stave churches can be found at several starting points, such as the stave church of Heddal (13th cent.), the largest preserved stave church.

23

Spring on the Sørfjord, with the Folgefonn peninsula in the background.

Folgefonn peninsula (walk 13–14):

The Folgefonna in the western Norwegian Hordaland, with its 212km^2, is the third-largest glacier in Norway, after Jostedalsbreen in Breheimen and Svartisen in Nordland. The plateau glacier, up to 34km long and 16km wide, is situated directly near the Hardangervidda on the Folgefonn peninsula, which is surrounded by the Hardangerfjord, Sørfjord and Åkrafjord. In no other part of Norway can you experience such rich contrasts in the countryside as on the Folgefonn peninsula: fjell, glacier and ocean, cirques and fertile valleys with diverse deciduous forests, mountain streams and rivers rich with trout and salmon. The parks at the Renaissance palace of the Rosendal Baronie accent what a glorious, sunny climate dominates in the western part of the peninsula. As a walking, ski tour, glacier walking, bathing, sunbathing, mountain biking and fishing paradise, the Folgefonn peninsula offers practically unlimited opportunities on an almost year-round basis.

This beautiful area has been inhabited since the last Ice Age, which ended about 10,000 years ago. Rock drawings, burial hills and other prehistoric traces, especially from the Bronze Age on, can be found in great numbers. The rock, largely granite and quartzite, breaks through the glacier in only a few spots, e.g. on the Holmaskjera (1565m). The highest elevation of the glacier, which has been exposed to strong dynamic forces in the last decades, is the Fonnanuten, with approximately 1662m. Walks over the Folgefonna enjoy a long tradition, because, until the arrival of efficient steam ships, it was much less time-consuming to travel from west to east or east to west by crossing the glacier than by rowing or sailing around the entire peninsula. Starting in the 1850's, the Folgefonna and its picturesque glacial falls, were discovered by British and German tourists, who were led over the ice by glacier guides, beginning in Odda. This wave of tourism experienced a significant upswing about 100 years ago, following the bold »North Land Trips« of German Emperor Wilhelm II., which was covered in detail by the press. In the 1890's, the German North Land Association (Nordlandverein) in Hamburg provided financing to have a riding path built from the Bondhus-elva valley to the vantage point called Breidablikk (»far view«) at the foot of a glacial tongue in the north-west of the Folgefonna. This path still exists today under the name »Keiservegen« (Emperor's Way) (see walk 14), and enables one of the most impressive landscape climbs to the Folgefonna. Thanks to the high elevation of the ice field, there is an unequalled panorama, which includes the Hardangervidda, with the striking Hårteigen in the east, as well as Hallingskarvet and Hardangerjøkulen in the north-east, as well as the multifarious island world in the west.

After completion of the Emperor's Way, the currently most frequented starting points were established as starting points for glacier tours on the Folge-

Boats in the harbour of Nordheimsund.

fonna: the unstaffed cabin Breidablikk (1332m) and the somewhat higher, self-serviced hut Fonnabu (1449m); the self-serviced Holmaskjerbu (1560m) is situated roughly east of these two huts on an island of rock surrounded by ice. Further starting points include the Buerdalen valley near Odda in the south-east of the peninsula, and the town of Tokheim, near Odda, from which a tourist riding path was also established to the glacier 100 years ago.

On the north edge of the glacier, on land belonging to the community of Jondal, the Folgefonna Summer Ski Centre can be found. Like the other glaciers in Norway, the Folgefonna May only be crossed by groups with glacier experience and the corresponding equipment. The Norwegian mountain association DNT and local glacier groups offer glacier courses and tours.

Hallingskarvet (walk 22–23)

The Hallingskarvet mountain crest rises east of the Hardangerjøkulen glacier and north of the Hardangervidda. It is visible from almost everywhere, and offers a tremendous view in all directions. Due to its unspoilt state and beautiful countryside, it is on the recommendation list of areas to be named as national parks. The crest (skarv = bare rock), covered with residual glacier and several patches of snow, even in summer, stretches from the winter sport centre **Geilo** 35km north-westward, peaks at **Folarskardnuten** (1930m) and rises steeply, especially in the south, up from the Ustedalen, but is like a plateau in the upper area and, with the exception of scree and boulders, is readily accessible.

Hardangerjøkulen (walk 23)

The Hardangerjøkulen, with its 78m^2, is the fifth-largest glacier in Norway, and ever since the opening of the railway line Bergensbanen (1909), one of the largest tourist attractions in the country. The plateau glacier is situated between the Hardangervidda and the Hallingskarvet mountain ridge at an elevation of up to 1862m. The main starting point for glacier tours is the winter sport centre Finse on the Bergensbahn. Hikers are warned not to access the Hardangerjøkulen without an experienced guide, because it is subject to strong dynamic forces (crevasses!).

Hardangervidda (walk 17–21 and 48)

The Hardangervidda, much of which is under national park protection, at over 9000km^2, is the largest plateau in Europe. It rises on the border of west and east Norway, and peaks at the partially-glacial Sandfloeggi (1719m); its most famous mountain is the rocky colossus of Hårteigen (1690m). Only a few parts of the gneiss and granite plateau, with an average 1200–1400m elevation, extend down to the forest zone.

In the west, the Sørfjord and Eidfjord, two tributaries of the Hardangerfjord, border the Hardangervidda; in the north, the glacier Hardangerjøkulen and

Cotton grass near Tinnsjø lake in eastern Hardangervidda.

ridge Hallingskarvet rise; in the east, the Uvdal and Numedal valleys form the boundary; in the south, the Haukelifjell and the area of the Totak and Møsvatn lakes make up more or less distinctive borders. The term »vidda« – related to the English »wide« – indicates a plateau with moorland, lakes, heath vegetation and glacially-rounded hills; this is especially true of the middle and eastern parts, crossed by fertile valleys.

In the south-west, on the other hand, where the highest peaks rise up from partially-glacial mountains, the terrain is fissured. In the waterfall-rich west, the plateau breaks off steeply to over 1000m at the Sørfjord, the eastern ridge of the Hardangerfjord.

Jæren (walk 1)

Jæren, on the south-western coast of Rogaland, is one of the most historical, affluent, and climatically favourable countrysides of Norway. There is not a single month in which the temperature sinks below an average of 0° in the Jæren flatlands.

This fertile outlying district – the name comes from the old Norwegian »jadar« = edge – between Randaberg near Stavanger in the north and the sandy beaches of **Ogna Bay** in the south was the starting point for Norwegian vikings who settled Ireland, Shetland, Greenland and Iceland. From the 18th century, Jæren was the granary of Norway; today, it is one of the most significant milk and cheese producers in northern Europe. After beginning offshore activities in Ekofiskfelt in the 1980's, the former bishopric seat **Stavanger** advanced to an oil metropolis as well as the fourth-largest city of the nation.

Seventy kilometres of the diverse coastline, with sandy beaches and dunes not typical of Norway, have been designated as the conservation area **Jærstrendene** – a refuge for plants and birds, as well as beach-going holiday-makers. **Orrevatnet** Lake, near the coast, and **Orresanden** Beach near Jærens rev, with 250 registered species, make up one of the most significant bird reserves of Norway. Between Orrevatnet and **Frøylandsvatnet** lake, located a few kilometres to the east, the ritual mountain **Tinghaug** (102m), surrounded by finds from the Bronze and Iron Age, surges up as one of the best viewpoints.

Generally, a number of relics of ancient times are found in Jæren, of the most remarkable being grave mounds and early medieval stone crosses. Walk 1 on **Synesvarden** (360m) in Upper Jæren offers an impressive vista. In these deserted highlands, characterised by heath, moorland, meadows and small lakes, we also witness a modern characteristic of the countryside: the kilometre-long gathered stone wall – made of collected stones – created as plot boundaries around 1900 during the last great land reallocation and common land division. This barren countryside was described in the naturalistic novels of Jæren writers Alexander Kielland (1849–1906) and Arne Garborg (1851–1924).

Jotunheimen (walk 24, 26–32 and 49)
Jotunheimen – literally »the home of the giants« – peaking in the **Galdhøpiggen** (2469m), is the highest mountain massif of northern Europe, the best developed with huts and paths and most frequently visited mountain hiking region in Scandinavia. It rises on the border between eastern and western Norway, and displays the characteristic relief forms of both parts of the country: the glacially-formed plateaux, with their rounded hills in the east are typical »Nordic« walking areas (on skis, too: »Nordic« cross-country); the folded and glacier-covered »alpine« west, on the other hand, is more challenging for mountaineers, and its Hurrungane is one of the most famous Norwegian climbing areas.

The immediate vicinity of alpine peaks and nordic rounded hills, of idyllic lakes, glaciers and fertile valleys, make this mountain chain one of the most diverse mountain countrysides of Europe.

The Jotunheimen mountain range, at approximately 2500km^2, is about as large as the German state of Saarland, or as large as Voralberg or Tessin. In 1980, 1140m^2 of the central high-mountain range were placed under protection as a national park. Adjacent to the national park is the Utladalen conservation area (300km^2).

In the Rondane mountain range: The Høgronden rises to the extreme left, to its right is the double-peaked Midtronden and the pyramids of the Digerronden.

Rondane (walk 34–37 and 50)

The Rondane mountain range (2178m), whose highest peak is Rondslottet in eastern Norway, is, after the Jotunheimen mountains, the most frequented mountain walking area in Norway. In 1962, it was placed under protection as the first national park of Norway: an ensemble consisting of gorge-like, deep valleys, moraine terraces and dead-ice holes, ridges between cirques with residual glaciers, fertile canyons, plant oases and a few pine forests, as well as Rondvatnet lake in the heart of the range. This mountain range, whose relief was formed by the Ice Age, is bordered on the west by Gudbrandsdalen, and in the north, Grimsdalen forms the boundary to Dovrefjell; on the other side of the River Atna in the east, the mountain area Alvdal Vestfjell ascends, and in the south, the Ringebufjellet borders the Rondane.

The Rondane range consists of slated sparagmite, a brittle type of sandstone that only allows a sparse growth of plants. The high-mountain region, with no vegetation except for lichen, is totally covered by slate and scree from an elevation of about 1400m. The carpets of reindeer lichen supply the zone between the tree line (approximately 1000m) and the boulder zone a yellowish-white to sulphur-green appearance.

Ryfylkeheiene (walk 2, 3, 10 and 11)
The wholly diverse fjord and mountain terrain of Ryfylke encompasses the catchment area of the widely branched-out Boknafjord, including the islands and the fjell areas known as the **Ryfylkeheiene** in eastern Rogaland at the transition area to Setesdalsheiene. To the north, the Haukelifjell borders the Ryfylkeheiene; the countrysides of Dalane and Jæren are located to the south. The highest elevation of the Ryfylkeheiene, which is characterised by a succession of dramatic rock scenery, gently rippled plateaux, spacious moorland and heath terrain, as well as deeply carved valleys and rounded mountaintops, and in which picturesque waterfalls, such as the **Månafossen** (walk 2), can be found, is the usually snow-covered **Snønuten** (1606m), above the Kyrkjesteindalen in the **Suldalsheiene** in the north-east. The Ryfylkeheiene mountains are divided into several individual mountain ranges, among which the Suldalsheiene and the **Saudafjella** are the most widely known. Above the Saudafjord, from which the name comes, rises the **Hustveitsåta** (1188m), which, among other things, is famous for its abundance of plants. Further to the north-east, the highest elevation, the mighty **Kyrkjenuten** massif (1602m), can be found adjacent to the wonderful mountain area of the **Berdalstindane** (walk 12) in the east. The most famous walking and climbing areas of the Ryfylkeheiene are located further to the south, on the legendary **Lysefjord**, from which the rocky spur **Prekestolen** (walk 3) and the almost 1000m high granite massif **Kjerag** (see walk 3) drop straight down.
In recent years, the Ryfylkeheiene, striped by several marked walking routes, and one of the most well-known wild-reindeer grazing areas in Norway, have been exposed to considerable damage through the energy industry, which set up a number of reservoirs and blasted utility roads into the fjell. The largest water reservoir of all of Norway is the 82km^2 large Blåsjøen, in whose vicinity the panoramic **Napen** surges upward (walk 11). The area south of the Lysefjord has been almost untouched by activities of the energy industry: The **Frafjordheiene**, which have been recommended to be made into a national park, and through which walk 2 leads, are located there. On walk 10, covering several days, we cross the border between Ryfylkeheiene and Haukelifjell.

Setesdal (walk 4, 5, 8 and 9)
The Setesdal, through which the Otra flows, is a silversmith handcraft centre, and one of the most naturally beautiful, primeval, and well-known valleys in Norway. From **Byglandsfjord** lake, a well-frequented rafting centre, the valley, surrounded by high, steep gneiss cliffs, runs over 100km northward,

On Lysefjord in the Ryfylkeheiene.

After an ascent through the Mjågeskor, the view falls back on the Store Bjørnevatn lake in the eastern Setesdalsheiene (Austheiene).

and flows into the source area of the Otra in the Haukelifjell, while two of the most significant walking and cross-country ski areas in southern Norway stretch along both sides of the valley: The **Setesdalsheiene** in the west, and the **Austheiene** in the east are composed of panoramic mountains and deeply-cut valleys, plateaux with strong relief areas containing countless lakes, bogs and reindeer grazing areas. Due to the perpendicular cliffs and the uninhabited plateaux on both sides, the Setesdal was largely cut off from the rest of the world right up into the 19th century, and has retained many old customs.

Telemark (walk 6–7, 44 and 46–48)
The southern Norwegian Fylke Telemark, the birthplace of modern skiing, stretches over 15,315km² from the Skagerrak coast to the eastern Hardangervidda, its capital is Skien. The mostly wooded, valley-rich medium mountain range countryside reaches its highest elevation, at 1881m, in Gaustatoppen (walk 47). Lifjell (walk 46), and Blefjell (walk 44) represent the most distinct individual mountains. The Lifjell rises above the Heddal, in which the largest preserved stave church is located. The multi-leg walk 48 leads along

the border of Telemark and Buskerund from Blefjell to the eastern Hardangervidda.

In addition to Lifjell and Blefjell, which, like the Gaustastock, prominently ascend over the tree line as fjell areas, there are a number of technically easy walking opportunities in Telemark, through idyllic forest and lake areas. The walk to the Troll Caves (walk 6), in that area which leads into the Setesdalsheiene, is one of the mainly easy walks. The beautiful walk around Ravnejuvet (walk 7) also leads through primarily primeval forest. Another interesting destination is the magical Nissedalen (Gnome Valley). As the birthplace of modern skiing (»Telemark Swing«), Telemark is a popular winter sport area. The sunny Telemark coast is also worth a visit: It is the origin of the Sørland coast, abounding in bays, with its skerry utopias and picturesque harbour towns.

Typical storehouses (Stabbur) in Austbø (Telemark).

1 On Synesvarden, 360m

Panoramic walk high above Jæren

Store Vandavatnet – Steinkjerringa – Synesvarden – Gauleksvarden – Vandavatnet

Location: The community of Hå lies south of Stavanger in the south-western Norwegian Fylke Rogaland in the agricultural area of Jæren. A suburb is Nærbø, whose dairy is one of the largest cheese producers in northern Europe.

Starting point: The hiking parking area of Steinkjerringa (210m), east-south-east of Nærbø. On Riksvei 44, Stavanger – Nærbø – Flekkefjord, turn off between Nærbø and Brusand onto Riksvei 504 in the direction of Varhaug; at the end of the town of Varhaug,

turn right in the direction of Hålland, later to the right once again in the direction of Hålland, lastly, at the fork, go straight to a field path to the signposted car park.

Walking times: Vandavatnet – Synesvarden, 2 hrs., Synesvarden – Vandavatnet, 2 hrs.; total time: 4 hrs. (11km).

Ascent: 200m.

Grade: The paths partially lead through boggy terrain; despite being well marked, a good sense of orientation is needed.

Map: TK 50, p. 1212 III Nærbø.

With a splendid view beyond the meadows and fields of Jæren to the coast and the sea, as well as to the mountains of southern Rogaland, this walk leads rather comfortably through wide meadows and moorland up to the panoramic hilltop of Synesvarden.

Starting from the **Steinkjerringa car park**, we follow the field path a short way up, and at the turnoff, turn right in the direction of »Steinkjerringe«, following the *blue* markers. The field path ends after a few metres at **Store Vandavatnet** lake.

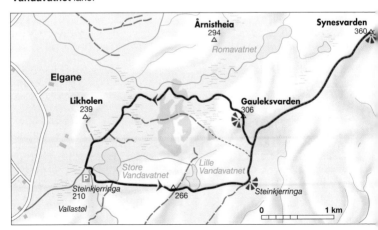

From Gauleksvarden, the view stretches up to Synesvarden.

We cross its outflow over a bridge and walk toward the forest. There, we use the steps to climb over a livestock fence, and follow the *blue* markers on a path through pine wood.

Soon, the path merges into a trail which lead left to the lake. At the end of the lake, the *blue* marker changes to a path on the right between young pine trees. At the end of the plantation, we climb over another livestock fence and are now in the conservation area. The panoramic path leads through the extensive, hilly, partially boggy meadowland, and on past **Lille Vandavatnet** lake, reaching the **Steinkjerringa** (Stone Wench), with an excellent panoramic location – even Synesvarden can be seen – : in 1926, the sitting statue of a »wench«, which was meant to personify Norway, was placed on a huge rock looking toward Jæren.

From the statue, we follow the *blue* markers up to a private hut, and turn there at the turnoff in the path halfway to the right. We later follow a gathered stone wall and reach the panoramic summit of **Synesvarden** (360m), on which there is now a wonderful view to the north.

From this peak, we go back along the same path (after crossing the stone wall on the right!) to the turnoff at the private hut, and here, with the *blue* markers on the right, continue up to the **Gauleksvarden** (306m) – another panoramic rest area. From the Gauleksvarden, we follow the *blue* markers in a rough west-northwesterly direction toward »Vandavatnet«; only traces of the trail are visible, but the trail markings are exemplary, and this passage possesses some of the finest natural beauty. The path is also well marked in the wood, before we come to a trail near a hut; it leads – still marked in *blue* – back to the starting point.

2   Valley walk in the Frafjordheiene

Two-day hut tour in the Fidjadalen

Månafossen – Fidjadalen – Blåfjellenden – Månafossen

Location: The community of Gjesdal lies on both sides of the inner Høgsfjord in the south-western Norwegian Fylke Rogaland, south-east of Stavanger.

Starting point: Bus stop and car park with a fee Eikeskog gården (120m) in Frafjorddalen. There are signs on Riksvei 45 for the very steep, panoramic pass road into the Frafjorddalen.

Walking times: Månafossen – Blåfjellen a good 5 hrs., return route 5 hrs., total time: 10 hrs. (28km).

Ascent: 600m.

Grade: A marked path with a few damp and rocky parts. The high route cited as an alternative is unmarked and can only be walked by experienced mountain walkers.

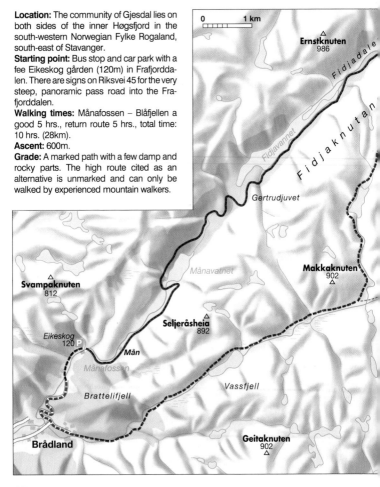

Hut: Blåfjellenden (600m), STF self-serviced hut (without provisions) with 18 berths.
Map: TK 50, p. 1312 IV Frafjord.
Alternative route: For an alternative return route, turn onto the unmarked path up into the fjell behind the first hut (Fidjastølen). After crossing the steep valley flank, parts of which are boggy, it passes by several small lakes over the panoramic Heiene plateau and leads steeply back into the valley. The plateau is an old reindeer grazing area.

From Månafossen, the highest waterfall in Rogaland at a 90mvertical drop, this valley walk leads through the expansive Fidjadalen through the Frafordheiene to the self-serviced hut Blåfjellenden.

From the car park at **Eikeskog gården**, we follow the *red T* markers upwards. The path is so steep and difficult, that chains have been attached to the rocks for a hold. The hard work is rewarded by marvellous views of the **Månafossen**. The waterfall rushing down through the steep step between the Frafjord and Fidja valleys has

Along this stream, wide in places, are idyllic places to pitch a tent.

The climb is accompanied by the roar of the Månafossen; above, the cliffs over the Fidjadalen.

After the steep ascent, the Fidjadalen can be viewed in almost its full length; halfway to the right is the Mån hut.

made this spot a tourist attraction; but just a short distance above is the start of the mostly pristine **Fidjadalen**, through which our walk leads to the Blåfellenden hut in the heart of the Frafjordheiene.

From the first hut on (**Mån**), there are no more unauthorised campfire spots; the relatively high valley is green and fertile, there are no birch woods, limited amount of moorland, and lakes are inviting for an ice-cold swim. Mån, and later, other huts, bear witness to earlier attempts to settle in this area. In between, wild clambering is called for, such as in the rocky chaos of a fallen mountain – marked however, in extreme detail with the *red T* symbols – behind which we reach **Månavatnet** lake.

Here, our route leaves the valley floor and leads along a wooded, steep escarpment north-west of the lake, before the markers lead us back down. The name **Huldrahaugane** indicates the fact that elf-like creatures live in this valley.

Directly beyond it, the **Gertrudjuvet** gorge opens up; then we walk along the stretched-out **Fidjavannet** lake toward the **Blåfjellenden** farm (600m), which was deserted in 1850 and now serves as a self-serviced hut. The hut is located on an expansion in which several valleys come together. However, there is no path connecting them. As long as the hut is not occupied by a class of schoolchildren or a group of hunters fond of drinking, you can take an enjoyable rest here and explore the surroundings.

3   On the Prekestolen spur, 600m

To the »Pulpit« above Lysefjord

Prekestolhytta – Prekestolen – Prekestolhytta

Location: The community of Forsand is situated on the Lysefjord and Idsfjord in southwest Norwegian Fylke Rogaland, east of Stavanger, and, in addition to the rocky and mountainous areas along the Lysefjord, also encompasses the majority of the planned national park »Frafjordheia«.

Starting point: Car park (320m) near the Prekestolhytta. Access via Riksvei 13 Sandnes – Forsand – Jørpeland, and in Jøssang south of Jørpeland, turn onto the cul-de-sac to the Prekestolhytta.

Walking times: Prekestolhytta – Prekestolen a good 2 hrs.; return route 2 hrs., total time: 4 hrs. (8km).

Ascent: 400m.

Grade: Well marked paths with a few rocky passages; in the end, path is exposed.

Hut: Mountain Hotel Prekestolhytta (0m).

Map: TK 50, p. 1212 I Høle.

Tip: In addition to Prekestolen, the Kjerag massif, plunging almost 1000m in a practically vertical drop to the fjord, with its famous Kjeragbolten, a wedged boulder has developed into a second mountain-tourist attraction on Lysefjord ever since the opening of the Setesdal – Lysebotn pass road. The ascent (3 hrs.) is begun at the car park near Øygardsstolen; the TurK 80, Soldal – Setesdalsheiene, shows the route.

This naturally beautiful walk leads to Prekestolen, a 25 x 25m large spur which plunges vertically on three sides and in overhangs 600m down to the Lysefjord. Since one cliff wall limits the back of the spur, and access is done via a relatively narrow, unsecured belt, persons prone to vertigo will find no mental holds. There are also no railings preventing a 600-foot jump into the Fjord, so many a hiker's hearts flutter, while others sit on the edge and dangle their legs over the abyss.

The spur, formerly named »Høvlatonnå« by the natives, was discovered as an excellent walking destination in 1901 from the deck of a ship in the Lysefjord; in fact, its pulpit-like character can best be seen from the vantage

The Prekestolen is a dance-floor-sized spur 600m above Lysefjord.

point of Lysefjord (the Forsand – Lysebotn ferry). Ever since, the spur, known by the name »Prekestolen«, has had a superlative mountain-tourism career, and investors have been busy for years lobbying democratic institutions to provide an access opportunity for a fee to people who couldn't be bothered to make the 4-hour climb, to ensure the approval of the establishment of a landing pier and the construction of an elevator to the Prekestolen. Another lobby would like to see an aerial cableway to Prekestolen built. As long as these projects have not been achieved, the Prekestolen, despite large crowds, can be enjoyed as a wonderful place of serenity and lingering. However, on days where fair weather enables beautiful panoramas, there are so many people present that a travelling beverage stand is set up.

From the car park near the **Prekestolhytta**, the path, designated on signs, leads quickly up into the fjell, whereby there are several viewpoints at which to rest along the way. In the end, the path becomes roughly strewn with boulders, and then leads through an exposed spot over a belt of rocks to the **Prekestolen** (600m).

The view falls upon the 40-km long, legendary Lysefjord and beyond to the mountain terrain of the Frafjordheia, which plunges down to the fjord at the Kjerag in 1000-m walls. The fjell is accessible farther up via a stairway on the back of the plateau.

4   From Setesdal to Svarvarnuten, 1377m

Panoramic walk in the Setesdalsheiene

Berg (Valle) – Stavskardhytta – Svavarnuten – Berg (Valle)

Location: The church village of Valle, a centre of handicrafts (silversmithing) is situated in a Setesdal expansion surrounded by gneiss walls on the Otra in the Southern Norwegian Fylke Aust-Agder. Finds from archaeological digs indicate that the valley expansion was used as early as the Viking period. The Setesdal Museum can be found in Flateland, 8km towards the valley.

Starting point: parking bay (710m) near Berg, across from Valle on the right side of the valley at the end of the toll road »Hylesdalsvegen«. Access via Riksvei 9

Kristiansand – Valle – Hovden.

Walking times: Car park– Svarvarnuten 3 hrs., return route 3 hrs., total time: 6 hrs. (16km). Car park – Bossbu (without summit) 7 hrs. Bossbu – Auguntjørnstølen – car park 7–8 hrs. (19km).

Ascent: 700m

Grade: Marked path which, in wet weather, could be flooded in passages near the lakes. The ascent to the Svarvarnuten is unmarked, as is the path from Augustjørnstølen – Berg, and thus only recommended for experienced mountain hikers.

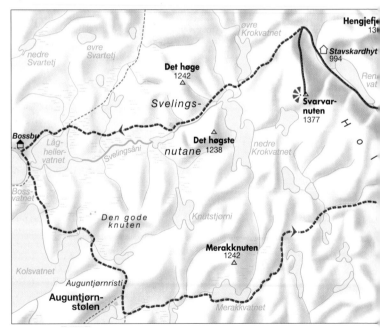

Huts: Stavskardhytta (994m), KOT self-serviced hut (10 berths, without provision). Bossbu (1030m), KOT self-serviced hut (34 berths); closed to hikers during the reindeer hunting season in winter.

Maps: TurK 80, p. Sirdal-Setesdalheiene; TK 50, p. 1413 II Valle (for the Bossbu variation, also 1413 III Rjuven).

Alternative route: From the summit back to the T-marked path, and along it (for about 6 more km) to the Bossbu hut at the shore of the large Bossvatnet lake (nice sandy beaches).

Continue on the T-marked path southward in the direction of »Svartenut«. After crossing the lake outflow bridge, head straight on at the fork and continue on until the path intersection at the Auguntjørnstølen mountain pasture. Here, we leave the T-marked path, branch on to the path to the left (eastward), and, without markings, turn back to the starting point.

From Valle in Setesdal, this comfortable walk leads through Setesdalsheiene, with its lakes, panoramic summits, and valleys. Among the highlights is the view from the Svarvarnuten; the Stavskardhytta is available for overnight accommodation. If you want to extend the walk to a three-day tour, continue to the Bossbu hut on the famous Bossvatnet lake, known for its sandy beaches, and return via the Auguntjørnstølen mountain pasture.

From the starting point near **Berg**, the path marked with a red T leads in the direction of »Bossbu« on the edge of a spring bog hollow westward. The destination is almost always visible: The Svarvarnuten rises straight above the cliff walls bordering the valley to the left.

Rennevatnet lake, whose outflow can be crossed over stepping stones, offers a pretty place to rest. A short distance further, we reach the **Stavskardhytta** (994m), and the path ascends the »Stave« pass (Stavskard); hut and pass are named after a property boundary »stave« on the pass.

Now, the T-marked path swings to the left, and we leave it in order to climb up to the **Svarvarnuten** (1377m) on an unmarked path; there are traces of a path. The excellent panorama which opens up on Svarvarnuten invites the hiker to extend the tour to include the chain of lakes at Bossvatnet.

5 On Bispevegen through the Austheiene

Panoramic plateau walk in Eastern Setesdal

Espetveit (Valle) – Rolvskvil – Finndalen – Stavvassdalen – Espetveit

Location: Valle, see walk 4.
Starting point: Espetveit (400m); turn off of Riksvei 9 north of Valle toward the direction of Tveitebø, then turn off in the direction of Espetveit. The path begins at the sign »Bispevegen«.
Walking times: Espetveit – Rolvskvil 3 hrs., Rolvskvil – Gamasbø 2 hrs., Gamasbø– Espetveit a good 3 hrs., total time: 8–9 hrs. (21km).
Ascent: 1200m.

Grade: Marked path with some steep inclines; wood and grassland, some passages rocky or full of scree.
Hut: Gamasbø (700 m, 4 berths, no provisions).
Maps: TurK 80, p. Sirdal-Setesdalsheiene, Setesdal Austhei Sør and Setesdal Austhei Nord; TK 50, p. 1413 ll Valle, 1413 I Urdenosi, 1513 IV Dalen, and 1513 lll Grossæ.

This plateau walk, full of woods and panoramas, leads on the Bispevegen (Bishop's Way) to the Austheiene. The highest point of the Bishop's Way, the legendary Rolvskvil Stack of Stones, offers a unique vista; then, we pass the Gamasbø hut on our way to Finndalen Valley before beginning the return route.

From the street in **Espetveit**, the sign »Bispevegen« indicates roughly an easterly direction uphill in the fjell birch zone. The way (path) bears its name

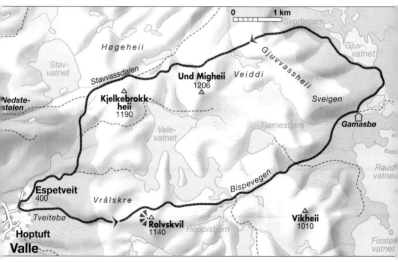

Rocky mountains above sparse forest – the Setesdalsheiene.

because, right up into the 19th century, it was supposedly used by bishops as a mountain passage between the Setesdal, Finndalen and Fyresdal Valleys.

After a good hour of ascending, the path marked with a *red T* leaves the forest zone and, with attractive views, leads up to the **Rolvskvil** stack of stones (1140m). Here, you have a wonderful view of the Austheiene on this side and the Vestheiene on the other side of the Setesdal Valley, as well as of the Valevatnet and Reppistjørn lakes, and others in the immediate vicinity. The area is supposedly named after a giant named Rolf, who had to spend a yule night here to atone for committing manslaughter.

Now, the *Bispevegen* leads panoramically down to an isthmus between the Valevatnet and Reppistjørn lakes, and then dives down into the fjell birch zone again, in which, above the large Raudvatnet lake, the small **Gamasbø** hut can be utilised for overnight accommodation. Raudvatnet lake is the home of the »church island« Kyrkjeholmen. A short distance later, at the turnoff in the path, we turn left to **Finndalen**, in which the oldest traces of settlement were found. The path remains on this side of the river, and Gjuvvatnet lake, and then leads westward with another panoramic view up to the Kahlfjell. At the fork in the path in **Stavvassdalen**, above Stavvetnet lake, we go down to the left (south), and are soon back to our starting point.

6 To the Troll Caves

Idyllic natural and cultural walk on Fyresvatnet

Kilegrand – Trollholene – Glomfoss – Kilegrend

Location: The mountain community of Fyresdal in West Telemark is situated on Fyresvatnet lake, on the east edge of the Setesdalsheiene (Austheiene).

Starting point: Car park at the school in Kilegrend. Access via Riksvei 41 Kristiansand – Kviteseid; at Tjønnefoss, turn onto Riksvei 355, look for the sign in Kilegrend »Grendehus / skule«.

Walking times: Kilegrend – Troll Caves 20 min, Troll Caves – Glomfoss 1½ hrs., Glomfoss – Kilegrend 10 min., total time: 2–3 hrs. (7km).

Ascent: 200m.

Grade: Easy walk following utility roads, partially along paths filled with undergrowth.

Refreshment: Øyne Camping.

Maps: TurK 80, p. Setesdal Austhei Sør; TK 50, p. 1513 ll Fyresvatnet and 1512 l Gjøvdal.

Tip: In the right weather: don't forget your bathing suit!

This idyllic forest walk in the south of Fyresvatnet Lake follows the natural and cultural trail *Øynuten rundt*, whose information boards are written in Norwegian and German. Among the highlights are the Troll Caves, the old school route, the Beaver Castle, the Glomfoss waterfall and the divine views of the lakes.

From the car park at the elementary school in **Kilegrend**, we follow the driveway up to the Riksvei. There, we turn right – led by a *blue* marker and the signs *Øynuten rundt*, as well as detailed information boards –, and cross the wooden **Bjønsundbruene** (Bear Sound Bridge) and arrive at the island around whose perimeter a nature trail can be found. Precipitous cliff walls, river bulges that resemble lakes, and diverse wood characterise this picturesque countryside.

At the second farm, we follow the »Trollholene« sign to the right up a steep path in surroundings resembling a primeval forest. The **Trollholene** (Troll Caves), which formed at the end of the last Ice Age about 10,000 years ago, are niches (half-caves), 3 to about 8-metres high and up to 4 metres deep, in the southern flank of the Øynuten, consisting of primeval wood. In the centre cave, which resembles a large hall and in which a good 50 people can fit, »Cave Church Services« have been held since 1911; at the entrance to the cave, which forms a natural amphitheatre, stands a large, wooden pulpit with a Christian cross. From the cave, one can look between the trees to see the waterfall of Krokane lake – a beautiful place for a rest.

From the Troll Caves, we return to the circular hiking trail. A short distance later, it turns into a path at **Krokane** lake, which served as a way to school for children from 1861 until the turn of the century. This rustic **School Way**, which, at first is populated by many bushes and subsequently is set up as a mountain path, ends at a forlorn farm on another lake; there is a chance to go bathing in the water here, too.

From the farm, we walk on a forest path to one of the numerous **beaver dens** (sign and steep path) on this lake, and then further into the forest, until we reach **Båttjørni**; there, we see remains of a landing pier from a time when the farms on the lake could not be reached by roads, but rather, when a boat sailed from farm to farm and to the church. A short distance later, our circular trail passes the serene **Øyne** campground (refreshment), passes through a tunnel, offers views of the former Glomfoss **sawmill**, and after crossing a dam, turns to the right onto the **Gamal Postveg**. Along this old postal route in the wood, we reach the panoramic cliffs above the **Glomfoss** waterfall, and return to the starting point.

At the Glomfoss waterfall.

7 To Ravnejuvet

Idyllic forest walk to the Raven Gorge

Eidsborg – Djupedalen – Ravnejuvet – Eidsborg

Location: The main town of the community of Tokke in West Telemark is Dalen, at the Bandak Reservoir, the end point of the Telemark Canal, which leads up from Skien. Next to the stave church of Eidsborg (approx. 1250), there is an outdoor museum, the Lårdal Bygdemuseum. The stave church dominates the countryside on a hill between two lakes high above the Tokka Valley. It was dedicated to Saint Nikolaus, whose statue was taken down to Eidsborg Lake every night on St. John the Baptist's Day up until 1780 and then bathed in connection with a formal procession.

Starting point: Parking bay (600m) in the right-hand curve above the Eidsborg stave church on Riksvei 45, Dalen – Høydalsmo.

Walking times: Eidsborg – Ravnejuvet a good 2 hrs., return route 2 hrs., total time: 4 hrs. (8km).

Ascent: 400m.

Grade: Marked trail, through partially boggy, then rocky forest terrain.

Maps: Natur- og Kulturkart 1:80,000, Tokke Kommune (available in the Tourist Informasjon in Dalen); TK 50 p. 1513 IV Dalen.

The fascinating thing about this partially very panoramic valley walk is the relatively seldom used, yet well marked trail through Djupedalen Valley, while the destination, Raven Gorge, famous for its unusual thermals, is also accessible by car (above) and is one of the outstanding tourist attractions of southern Norway. Along the path are several beautiful spots to pitch a tent.

At the parking bay on the curve above the **Eidsborg Stave Church**, we cross the national road (Riksvei 45), follow the »Ravnetjuvet« hiking trail signs gently downhill on a forest road, and go straight on at the crossroads, following *yellow direction arrows* and *orange* markers. Shortly after passing mountain pasture huts at the end of a field, the road turns into a path. At the next crossroads a short distance later, we follow the markers to the left, and walk upward in a sparse fjell birch forest, accompanied by the rushing of a stream.

After crossing a romantic mountain pine wood, our path leads through a boggy hollow with cotton-grass meadows and Norwegian raspberries, then we become surrounded once again by blueberry-rich pine wood, in which cliff walls surge up while our quiet, now rocky path, extends upward next to a mossy stream bed – marvellous.

If you cross the path, which traverses streams on stepping stones or make-shift wooden bridges several times, leave it a little and roam around, you will reach rocky ledges with ancient pines and an excellent view to the south of the Bandak Valley. Without leading above the tree line, the path continues at a moderate ascent up to 800m, and passes through the **Djupedalen** (Deep Valley), before the descent to **Ravnejuvet** begins: If light objects – bank-notes, tissues, love letters – are thrown into the gorge, up-currents will carry them back to the edge of the cliff or let them sail over the gorge.

On the cliff above the ascent to Ravnejuvet, there are several chances to enjoy the panorama of the heights beyond Bondak Valley.

8 Through Mjågeskor

Panoramic walk in the northern Austheiene

Bjørnevassthytta – Mjågeskor – Reidalsfjell – Bjørnevassthytta

Location: Valle, see walk 4.
Starting point: Bjørnevassthytta (800m) east
of Bykle on Riksvei 45.
Walking times: Bjørnevassthytta – Mjågeskor 1 hr., Mjågeskor – Reidalsfjell – Bjørnevasshytta 7 hrs., total time: 8 hrs. (20km).
Ascent: 600m.

Grade: In Mjågeskor, absence of vertigo
and sure-footedness are essential.
Hut: Bjørnevassytta, in the summer season
a staffed KOT hut (32 berths), outside of the
summer season, self-serviced.
Maps: TurK 80, p. Setesdal Asthei North;
TK 50, p. 1413 I Urdenosi.

This diverse panoramic walk leads past the Kyrelitjørnet moor bird sanctuary
and through isolated highland accentuated by lakes above the tree line.

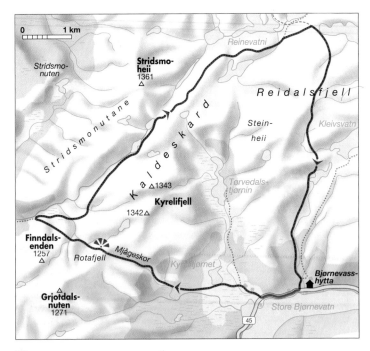

Higher up, ascent of the Mjågeskor requires an absence of vertigo.

From **Bjørnevasshytta**, the route, designated with *red T* markers, briefly follows the street along **Store Bjørnevatn** lake, and then branches off into the moorland and wet areas allocated as a bird protection area surrounding **Kyrelitjørnet** lake.

After passing old mountain pasture huts, we follow the markers though the Mjågeskor (mjå = narrow, skor = wind gap), a fairly steep diagonal crack in the flank of the cliff, up to 1.5m wide and only a few centimetres deep. The very panoramic ascent ends where the crack widens. Up to the left, there is a small lake which is perfect for a rest with a view.

When the marked trail descends once again, (it leads to Bykle), we branch off to the right on the unmarked path, and follow the stream valley upward, cross the watershed, and behind it, continue gradually downstream. Before the **Reinevatni** lakes, we go to the right, until we once again join a *T*-marked main hiking trail. It leads to the south over the panoramic **Reidalsfjell** and then back to **Bjørnevasshytta**.

9 To the Sloaros plant oasis

Plateau walk above the northern Setesdal

Hovden – Sloaroshytta – Hovden

Location: Hovden (800m) is the most important holiday and winter sport centre in Setesdal Valley. Access via Riksvei 9 Kristiansand – Setesdal – Hovden – Haukeligrend.
Starting point: Hovden Alpinsenter (800m), signs on Riksvei 9.
Walking times: Hovden – Sloaros 5 hrs., return route 5 hrs., total time: 10 hrs. (29km).
Ascent: 1000m.
Grade: Despite the ascent, no special grade; part of the route is an old cart road.
Huts: A number of refreshment and accommodation opportunities in Hovden; Sloaroshytta (1045m), KOT self-serviced hut.
Maps: TurK 50, p. Hovden; TurK 100, p.

Etne-Saudafjella; TK 50, p. 1414 II Sæsvatn and 1414 III Breive.
Alternative routes: 1) At Gjuvshedderkollen, the path branches off down into Myrekvævdalen (3 hrs., approx. 9km there and back).
2) To get to the Storheller Runes, starting from the Sloaroshytta, we follow the route (7) in the direction of »Holmevasshytta«, and when the path slopes down to the western bay of Fisketjøm lake, turn left, arrive at the former Molybdän ore mine at Langvatn, and continue on the path past Storhedderhalsen to Storheller, above the Storheddervatnet (5 hrs., 15km there and back).

From the winter sport centre Hovden, this panoramic plateau walk leads to the lake landscape at the Sloarsoshytta in the northern Setesdalsheiene. From the hut, situated in a vegetation-rich environment, one can take several side-trips, such as to the lush Myrekvævdalen Valley and the Storheller Runes, an old hunting station with cave etchings (sun crosses, hunters with bows and arrows, runes) from the period around 1100–1150. The area, with numerous lakes, is also a popular fishing spot; you can obtain a fishing permit (Fiskekort) in Hovden.

From the large car park in front of the **Alpine Centre of Hovden**, we follow the foot and bicycle path a few meters in the direction of Riksvei 9, then turn left into the first farm way (a barrier with a »Do not enter« sign, a wooden sign indicating the direction of »Sloaros«), and soon discover, on an unsurfaced road ascending between fjell birch, a *red T* marker, which points out the rest of the route. Shortly before the road reaches a meadow at an farmhouse, our markers switch to the left, on a narrow, stony path which initially runs through fjell birch wood, then through the boundary zone of the moorland preserve **Vidmyr** (wide moor), and, at almost 1300m at the **Krosslosskardat** col, crosses the *Hardingvegen*, the historical fjell crossing from Breive to Røldal. Here, we leave the path, branch off to the right (to the north) onto the *T*-marked *Hardingvegen*, and follow it past cement relics from World War I, down to the lakes. From **Hardingskardet**, we can see the Sloaroshytta for the first time, then we reach the shore of the **Langvatn lake**, and follow it to the right to **Gjuvshedderkollen** hill, famous for its botanical treasures.

After passing a branch in the path, our route, following the shore area, swings to the left, and a short distance later, we are at the **Sloaroshytta** (1045m), on **Sloarosvatn** lake. In the vicinity of the hut, in addition to a rich assortment of flora, we also see countless traces of the Molybdän ore mining from the 18th century; even today, modern treasure hunters still search for the shimmering, metallic mineral.

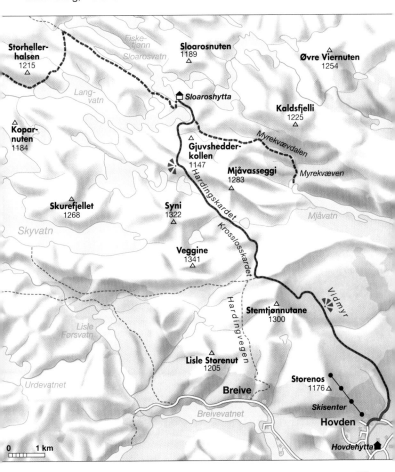

10 Through the Kvanndalen to the Haukelifjell

Five-day hut walk from Suldalsvatnet to the Haukelifjell

Roaldkvam – Kvanndalen – Haukeliseter – Holmevasshytta – Kvanndalshytta – Roaldkvam

Location: Suldal, see walk 11.
Starting point: The old village of Roaldkvam (70m) is situated at the eastern end of the Suldalsvatnet; accessible via Riksvei 13 Sand – Røldal, full of tunnels, at Nesflaten, turn in the direction of Bleskestad, in Roaldkvam straight on in the direction of Bleskestad and park where you can; the hiking trail begins at the first farm way on the left (no parking).
Walking times: Roaldkvam – Kvanndalshytta 5 hrs. (10km, 800m. alt.), Kvanndalshytta – Haukeliseter 8 hrs. (22km, 700m. alt.), Haukeliseter – Holmevasshytta 6 hrs. (16km, 400m. alt.), Holmevasshytta – Kvanndalshytta 5 hrs. (14km, 300m. alt.), Kvanndalshytta – Roaldkvam 4 hrs. (10km, 300m. alt.); total time: 28 hrs. (72km).
Ascent: 2500m.
Grade: The main demand is good physical

condition; there are some steep ascents and many passages of stone and scree.
Huts: Kvanndalshytta (661m), ST self-serviced hut (8 berths, no provisions). Haukeliseter, ST mountain hotel (1000m) with 110 beds and an addition opened year-round (30 berths, no provisions). Holmevasshytta (1130m), ST self-serviced hut (20 berths).
Maps: TurK 100, p. Etne-Saudafjella; TK 50, p. 1314 II Suldalsvatnet, 1414 III Breive and 1414 IV Haukelisæter.
Alternative route: At the path crossroads after the Tverråna bridge, go straight on to the Bleskestadmoen self-serviced hut (6 hrs. to hut, *T* markers), and from there on the next day, back to Roaldkvam (a good 3 hrs.), the last 5km of which on a seldom-used road ending in a cul-de-sac. At Sandvatnet, an option is to take the (private) factory road, which also leads back to the isolated valley.

With four hut stays, plan on almost a week for this grand valley and plateau walk at the transition from the Ryfylkeheiene to the Haukelifjell. At the beginning of july, there is no snow in the lower elevations, but on the Haukelifjell it is snow-melting season, so that it is best to wait until the end of july to walk this route.

In the village of **Roaldkvam**, with its buildings that are, to some extent, ancient, we switch at the first fork from the through-road in the direction of Bleskestad to the unsurfaced road diagonally to the left, and walk toward the forest. After only a few minutes, we reach the forest, and proceed through a gate there (please remember to close it behind you), and follow the direction sign »Kvanndalen« and the red-T markers diagonally to the right into the forest. In the woody Juvstøldalen, the road, which soon turns into a path, continues rather steeply uphill, leaves the forest zone and leads to the **Kvanndalshytta** (661m) in **Kvanndalen**, situated on a meadow below the Svultanuten. Now we are guided upward by the valley and the wide river Kvanndalsåna, which repeatedly spills over stairways of rock in the form of picturesque waterfalls. The *T*-marked path frequently passes old mountain pasture huts, then we reach the watershed at **Kistenuten** at almost 1200m, and walk through Ståvassdalen valley down to the **Ståvatn** reservoir, on whose opposite bank lies **Haukeliseter** (1000m).

From the mountain hotel, we follow the *T* at the shore of the lake back to the turnoff in the direction of Holmevasshytta, then follow the shore of the reservoir **Kjelavatn** to the south, walk downhill in the lake-rich Vassdalen until we reach the highest point in the Turistskardet at 1330m. Then, the *T* markers lead past the Fitjanuten and down to the **Holmevasshytta** (1130m) above the Holmavatnet reservoir. From Holmevasshytta, the path leads further to the south, with many scenic views, to the Sandvatnet reservoir, where, shortly after crossing the Tverråna bridge, we reach a turnoff: we turn right and follow the panoramic path back to the **Kvanndalshytta**. The last leg back to **Roaldkvam** is identical to the journey there.

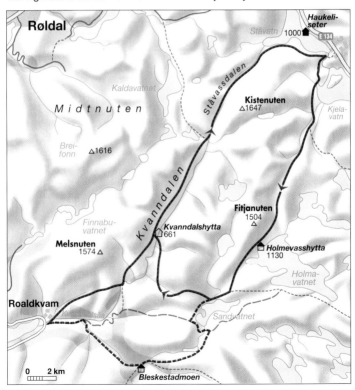

11 On panoramic Napen, 1350m

Magnificent panoramic mountain in Ryfylkeheiene

Parking bay – Napen – parking bay

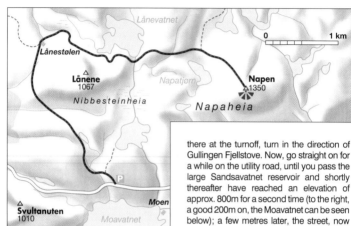

there at the turnoff, turn in the direction of Gullingen Fjellstove. Now, go straight on for a while on the utility road, until you pass the large Sandsavatnet reservoir and shortly thereafter have reached an elevation of approx. 800m for a second time (to the right, a good 200m on, the Moavatnet can be seen below); a few metres later, the street, now leading downhill, passes under a power line, and a few metres after that, we see a parking bay in the right-hand curve on the left; this is where the marked path begins.

Walking times: Parking bay – Napen almost 3 hrs., return route 2 hrs., total time: 5 hrs. (13km).

Ascent: 600m.

Grade: Sure-footedness, lack of vertigo, and a good sense of orientation; in the rocky and partially very steep terrain, there are several opportunities to lose one's way.

Maps: TurK 100 p. Etne-Saudafjella; TK 50 p. 1313 I Blåfjell.

Location: The Rogaland community of Suldal in the Ryfylke is situated on both sides of the 27-km long Suldalsvatnet and the River Suldalslågen; the main town is the ferry port Sand on the Sandsfjorden. Access via Riksvei 13 Sandnes – Sand – Røldal – Odda – Kinsarvik.

Starting point: Parking bay (approx. 780m) on the utility road to the Blåsjø reservoir. From the port town of Sand, drive down Riksvei 13 in the direction of Røldal, turn right to the winter sport centre Gullingen, and

This walk leads through majestic mountain scenery on to Napen, one of the panoramic summits of the Ryfylkeheiene.

From the **parking bay** on the Blåsjø water power plant road, we follow the path down to the stream rushing down from a gap in the cliff wall. Seen from below, we ascend left of the gap on the rocky mountain path identified by cairns and covered by slippery, stone chips. Soon, this steep zone ends, and, surrounded by green, we reach an inconspicuous turnoff (at which it is easy to get lost on the return route), at which we continue to the left, again seen from below. The path continually gains altitude, and soon a splendid panorama opens up of the snow-speckled mountains on the other side of the deep valley cut by the river Ulla.

Here, the path swerves up slightly to the right between tiny lakes, and hits somewhat confusing terrain, with bare, rocky ridges. Here, you must pay close attention to the cairns, because the route as a path is often hard to discern on the rock.

Passing a somewhat larger lake, we walk with a view to the flanks of the cliffs of the Nibbesteinheia, heading for its west side, where, at the panoramic mountain pasture **Lånestølen**, we come upon the southern route, marked with a *red T*, between the unstaffed hut Sandsa (to the left) and the Stranddalen hut (to the right), which is staffed in the summer; it will take another 2 hours (7km) to reach the Sandsa hut (1045m), and another 1½ hours (5km) to reach the Stranddalen hut (970m).

We follow the *T* markers to the right (north-east) in the direction of the Strandalshytta to the **Lånevatnet** and on to a turnoff, where the marked trail up **Napen** (1350m) begins, which offers an unequalled view of the Ryfylke-heiene and the Setesdalsheiene.

During the ascent to Napen, parts of which are very steep, the view falls on the deep valley cut by the river Ulla.

12 On Søre Berdalstinden, 1564 m

Over the Berdalstindane in the Saudafjella

Car park – Søre Tinden – car park

Location: Sauda on the Saudafjord is the centre of the community of the same name in the south-western Norwegian Fylke Rogaland.
Starting point: Car park (860m) at the obelisk monument for Knut Vesthassel on Riksvei 520 Røldal – Sauda; Riksvei 520 is a narrow pass road.
Walking times: Car park – Søre Tinden a good 2 hrs., return route 2 hrs., total time: a good 4 hrs. (10km).
Ascent: 800m.
Grade: Sure-footedness and knowledge of the weather; some of the terrain is very steep. Parts of the ascent may be covered with old snow, even in the middle of summer.
Maps: TurK 100, p. Etne-Saudafjella; TK 50, p. 1314 I Røldal and 1314 II Suldalsvatnet.

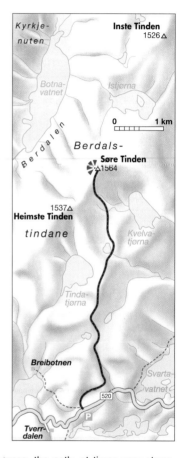

This great mountain walk leads onto Søre Tinden, the highest of the Berdalstindane high above the deeply cut trough valley, Berdalen. The ascent is well marked, however the markers must be followed exactly, as the partially steep terrain, with fallen rock, may be hard to follow, despite the relatively clear course of the route.

From the **obelisk monument**, we follow the national road a few metres down in the direction of Sauda, until we reach a spot marked with a cairn, where the trail marked with a *red T* branches off to the right and immediately leads to another turn-off, where we once again turn right. Along boulders and through cotton grass, the path, at times very steep, leads upward with a tremendous view.

View from the Berdalstindane to the west over the Saudafjella.

Above the first steep level, the trail continues to the right over a panoramic ridge covered with ferns, Lapland willows, cowberry and blueberry bushes, cotton grasses and Norwegian raspberries, and richly decorated with flowers: The impression gained on the pass that the fjell terrain only consists of scree and rock here is misleading.

Now, the path swings up to the left into a gap, and follows a stream steeply to a small lake surrounded by cliffs. If the view has been magnificent up to now – the mighty ridge of the Skaulen is an eye-catcher – it becomes even more magnificent on the rocks above the nameless lake which offer a good place to rest: a unique vista of the mountainous countryside beyond the deeply cut Berdalen.

Now, the path crosses a watershed, then continues with a grand vista past nameless lakes, before we reach the scree-covered, final sprint onto **Søre Tinden** (1564m): Almost the entire Saudafjella mountain landscape lies at your feet; only the mighty dome of the Kyrkjenuten (1602m) is somewhat higher.

13 Folgefonn peninsula

Mountain walk between glaciers and the sea

Uskedalen – Englafjell – Mannen – Uskedalen

Location: The community of Kvinnherad on the Hardangerfjord in Hordaland encompasses the western portion of the Folgefonn peninsula, and is one of the most attractive and naturally diverse skiing, mountain and water sport, walking and fishing holiday regions in southern Norway.
The largest town is the tourism centre of Rosendal, with the Rosendal Baronie, a Renaissance palace dating from the 18th century.

Starting point: Car park (10m) in Kvinnherad-Uskedalen at the turnoff to the campground and church on Riksvei 48, Bergen – Rosendal – Uskedalen – Skånevik.
Walking times: Uskedalen – Englafjell 3 hrs. (4km, 1200m. alt.), Englafjell – Jordsvatnet

1 hr. (2km, a good 400m. alt. descent), Jordsvatnet – Mannen almost 1 hr. (2km, 250m. alt.), Mannen – Uskedalen a good hour (5km, a mostly steep ascent), total time: 6 hrs. (13km).
Ascent: 1500m.
Grade: Sure-footedness, lack of vertigo, and good physical condition; parts of the route include very steep ascents and descents.
Accommodation: Huts and campground in Uskedalen.
Maps: TurK 100, p. Folgefjonna-Hardangerfjorden; TK 50, p. 1214 I Kvinnherad and 1214 IV Husnes.
Tip: Another worthwhile circular walk leads from Uskedalen eastward to Mannsvatnet and around the lake (4 hrs., 13km).

With a number of walking routes in picturesque mountain countryside, the sunny western part of the glacier-covered Folgefonn peninsula is one of the most diverse areas of southern Norway. Since the peninsula is embraced by arms of the Hardangerfjord, almost all routes include ascents which are considerable and steep; in return, during the ascent and on the summits, hikers are rewarded with unsurpassed panoramas of the Folgefonn plateau glacier, which reaches 1638m at its highest point, and of the beautiful Hordaland coast with its islands. The highest non-glacial mountain is the Melderskin (1426m) near Rosendal.

At the car park near the church in **Uskedalen**, the steeply towering mountain peaks of Englafjell and Mannen are visible. We follow the national road over the bridge, which crosses the stream flowing out of Uskedalen valley, then turn left immediately in the direction of »Musdalen«, down into the meadows, and walk straight on in the curve (sign: »Turveg«), now following the *blue* markers in the direction of »Englafjell«. Right afterwards, the road turns into a steep path which first leads through diverse wood, then, above the tree line, to the panoramic **Såta** (652m) and continues steeply up to the **Englafjell** summit (1200m).

Next, the partially steep descent leads westward to the **Lomatjørna** and **Jordsvatnet** lakes (777m). Here, there is the opportunity to descend through the Eikedalen, with a limited panorama (approx. 5km descent, parts of which are steep, which shortens the walk by a good hour); otherwise we climb up to the summit of **Mannen** (1013m), before beginning the extremely panoramic descent of approximately 1000 metres of altitude.

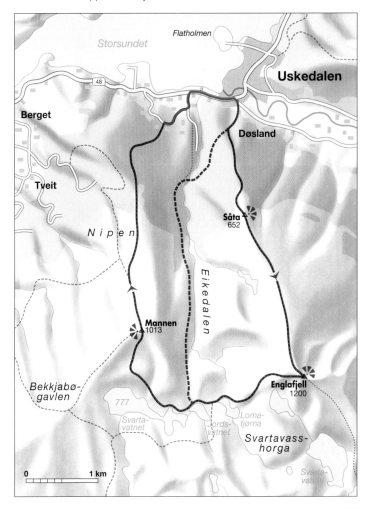

14 To the Bondhusbreen glacial falls

Impressive walk to Bondhusbreen

Sunndal – Bondhusvatnet – Bondhusbreen – Sunndal

Location: Kvinnherad, see walk 13.
Starting point: Car park (50m) in Kvinnherad-Sunndal.
Walking times: Sunndal – glacial lake 20 min., glacial lake – glacial falls a good hour, return route a good 1½ hrs., total time: 3 hrs (10km).
Ascent: 300m.
Grade: From the lake the route follows a stony path with wet spots in the last part.
Maps: TurK 100, p. Folgefjonna-Hardan-gerfjorden; TK 50, p. 1315 III Odda.
Alternative route: Shortly before reaching the glacial lake, the *red-T* markers branch off to the left, cross the river over a bridge and lead on the steep *Keiservegen* to the self-serviced Breidablikk hut (4 berths, no provisions; about 5 hrs., 7km, 1200m. alt.), which is located on the plateau, and Fonnabu (16 berths; almost one additional hour, 2km, 200m. alt.), both starting points for glacial walks.

This walk, displaying very impressive countryside, leads on a comfortable path to the glacial lake Bondhusvatnet, and continues on a rather stony path to the glacial falls of Bondhusbreen.
At the car park, we cross the glacial river **Bondhuselva** over a bridge, and walk upwards in the deeply-cut **Bondhusdalen** valley to **Bondhusvatnet**, where the glacial falls become visible.

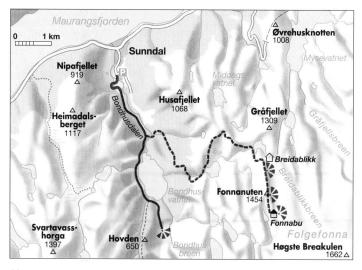

The Bondhusbreen glacial falls.

Above the western shore of the lake, a stony path leads to the waterfalls of the **Plyttelva**. We cross it over bridges and then follow the *red ring* above the steep bank. Shortly before reaching the alluvial cone, upon which the Bond-huselva leaves deposits on its way to the lake, our path swings up to the right, and, after a boggy part, a marvellous vista of the thundering ice mass of **Bondhusbreen** opens up. For safety reasons, we do not recommend walking further to the glacial tongue.

15 On Tysnessåta, 753m

On the highest peak of a holy island

Myrdal – Buskaret – Tysnessåta – Myrdal

Location: The community of Tysnes is situated in the western Norwegian Fylke Hordaland on the island of Tysnesøya, between Bjørnafjord and Hardangerfjord.

Starting point: Car park at Myrdal (200m), indicated in signs in Myrdal as »Tysnessåta car park« on Riksvei 49 Norheimsund – Tysnes.

Walking times: Myrdal – Tysnessåta 1 hr., return route 1 hr., total time: 2 hrs. (4km).

Ascent: 600m.

Grade: Lack of vertigo in terrain which, in spots, is very steep.

Map: TK 50, p. 1215 III Fusa.

Seven paths, including our shortest and steepest, lead from all directions toward the panoramic Tysnessåta, the highest elevation of the island Tysnesøya between Bjørnafjord and Hardangerfjord. Up to the Middle Ages, the island was called Njardarlog (Njörd's Holy Place), and was a cultural centre of the Vanic/Germanic god of fertility and peace, Njörd-Nerthus. Countless toponyms are reminiscent of the old religious function: Vevatnet (Shrine Lake), Prestesætra (Priests' Pasture), Hovlandsnuten (Temple Land Mountain), Tysnes (tongue of land of the Germanic God of Heaven, War, and Ting, Tyr), Gudøya (God Island). We would have liked to have presented the route indicated in a dotted line on the topographical map over the Priests' Pasture, but it is obstructed. Thus, there are seven paths to this steep mountain, but they are not connected with each other. A rough overview map at the starting point shows the seven routes, one of them to the Hovlandsnuten. Our ascent through the Buskaret is identified as »svært bratt« (very steep).

At the car park at the **Myrdal** farm, we climb over a livestock fence and follow a steep, stony mountain-pasture road, lush with vegetation, upwards. Before reaching the next livestock fence, we switch to a stony mountain trail on the right, which leads up along side of the fence, before we go through a gate in the fence and arrive at a panoramic mountainside path. The path, occasionally marked with a *red T* and which should not be lost, leads steeply upward between juniper, Lapland willows, birch and ferns in the flowery, steep slope of the gorge valley **Buskaret**, while to the lower left, in another gorge-like, cut-out rocky bed, the **Steinelva** rushes by. Before the terrain flattens out on top, the steep mountainside path crosses two spots which could be conside-

Short, steep, and panoramic is the way through which our trail to the summit leads.

red exposed; then we reach a panoramic ledge with a view northward to the island landscape in the Bjørnafjord.

The path, which from here on is well marked, now partially leads in the line of slope, steeply, but unexposed, downward in a steep escarpment interspersed with rocks that, if you turn around, continually allows for a breathtaking panorama eastward toward the Folgefonn peninsula. When the terrain begins to flatten, we can also enjoy the view of the island to the south, and once we reach the stone marker of the **Tysnessåta** (753m), the view expands to include the islands in the west, and beyond to the open sea. The summit register is located in a tin box inside the stone marker. From the white curve of the Folgefonn glacier, the view extends to the neighbouring island, Stord, and in the north, to the pointy Ulriken, the favourite mountain of the Hanseatic city, Bergen.

16 Vesoldo, 1046m

The sun's throne over the Hardangerfjord

Byrkjenesvatnet – Vesoldo – Byrkjenesvatnet

Location: The community of Kvam is located in the western Norwegian Fylke Hardaland north of the Hardangerfjord. The centre is the settlement, resembling a town, of Norheimsund. Access via Riksvei 7 Bergen – Norheimsund – Geilo – Hønefoss.
Starting point: Parking bay (200m) at the Byrkjenesvatnet: In Norheimsund, turn onto Riksvei 551 and drive along the Strandebarmsbukta to Fosse, where you turn onto the mountain road in the direction of Haukås. After a while, turn off right in the direction of Tordal (Tordalsvegen), and lastly, follow the unsurfaced toll road »Byrkjenesvegen« to the hiking sign »Vesoldo« above the lake shortly before the high-tension wires.
Walking times: Byrkjenesvatnet – Vesoldo a good 2 hrs., return route 2 hrs., total time: 4 hrs. (10km).
Ascent: 800m.
Grade: Starts out as a comfortable forest path, higher up it becomes steep and full of scree.
Maps: TurK 100, p. Folgefjonna-Hardangerfjorden; TK 50, p. 1215 I Norheimsund.

This forest and fjell walk leads to one of the mightiest mountains over the Hardangerfjord, the double-peaked Vesoldo, which drives into the fjord from the north like a peninsula. The prefix »Ve-« (sacred place, shrine) indicates that it is a holy site, as do the rock etchings, Bauta memorial stones and grave mounds along its river.

Its silhouette looks most striking on the opposite shore of the Hardangerfjord, in Herand, where 85 of the most interesting rock drawings in western Norway were discovered: These images, made around 3000 years ago, show, among other things, mover 20 woman and ithyphallic men who, during a hierogamic fertility ritual, look westward to the »sacred sun mountain«, Vesoldo, behind whose frontage the sun sets on the evenings of the equinox.

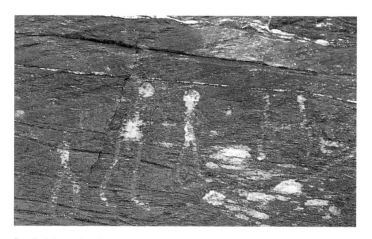

Detail of the rock etchings of Kalhalgen in Bakke.

From the parking bay above the **Byrkjenesvatnet**, we follow the hiking sign »Vesoldo« upwards on a path in the wood. Shortly before a small waterfall, the path swerves to the right and now follows the hillside gently upward, where picturesque views between the trees offer glimpses of the lakes and surrounding mountains.

The grassy trail leads along the slope between juniper, birch and ferns, between rocks, pine, spruce, hazelnut bushes, blueberries and bell-flowers – a beautiful hiking trail which becomes smaller and rockier as soon as we have passed the Nauthellerskår turnoff. Finally, we turn off to the left, now gaining altitude faster, pass the **Lingheller** mountain pasture huts, cross the waterfall stream, and immediately turn off to the right at the hut.

After a short, steep ascent, the mountain path leaves the forest zone and, offering a tremendous vista of the Hundsryggen, continues toward the panoramic summit of **Vesoldo** (1046m): over 1000 metres above the Harangerfjord, the view sweeps over to the Folgefonn peninsula, towering precipitously up from the arm of the sea and covered in the curve of the plateau glacier.

Dead east, we can make out the Bakke rock-drawing bay below, with the Samlen dome jutting out like a peninsula into the fjord. The view of the Hardangervidda is somewhat blocked by the Gråfjell on the northern Folgefonn peninsula, but the highest, snow-capped mountains are in view, and to the north of them, we see the Hardangerjøkulen glacier, while in the near west, the glacier-covered Tveitakvitingen is visible.

17 From Sørfjord to Nosi, 900m

Panoramic and bathing walk on the western edge of the Hardangervidda

Lofthus – Nosi – Opesjovatnet – Lofthus

Location: The community of Ullensvang, Norway's largest fruit-growing area, lies in the Fylka Hordaland on both sides of the Sørfjord, and encompasses the north-western Hardangervidda as well as the northeast Folgefonn peninsula. The administrative centre is the ferry port Kinsarvik. In Ullensvang, you can find the hut in which Edvard Grieg composed, which is set up as a museum. In Aga, on the western shore of the Fjord, the outdoor museum Klyngetun can be found, with over 50 old houses.

Starting point: Campground (100m) in Ullensvang-Lofthus; Riksvei 13, Røldal –

Odda – Kinsarvik.

Walking times: Lofthus – Nosi almost 3 hrs. Nosi – Opesjovatnet 2 hrs., Opesjovatnet – Lofthus 3 hrs., total time: 8 hrs. (18km).

Ascent: 1200m.

Grade: Good physical condition.

Maps: TurK 100, p. Hardangervidda Vest; TK 50, p. 1315 I Ullensvang.

Alternative routes: 1) Continuation to the DNT self-serviced hut, Torehytta, 8 hrs., 21km from the eastern point of our circular walk. **2)** Continuation to Hårteigen from Torehytta (see walk 19), 2 hrs., 4km, almost 400m alt.

This excellent day-long walk leads steeply up to Nosi, a panoramic mountain »nose« on the western edge of the Hardangervidda, then in the national park,

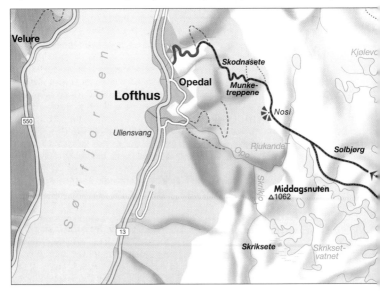

The Sørfjord between the Hardangervidda and the Folgefonn peninsula.

along several lake-like bulges in the river Opo, to Opesjovatnet lake.

In order to gain an overview of the grandiosity of the terrain through which the ascent leads, the terrace of the restaurant in Velure on the west side of the Sørfjord is an ideal spot: The western edge of the Vidda, parts of which break up steeply in the form of a wall, recedes back here in a harmonic, concave form, and two gigantic waterfalls spill through the upper portion of this approximately 900-m high hollow – the Rjukande (the Smoking One) rushes down from the left, and from the right, the Skrikjo (the Screamer) thunders over the cliff walls. Both join to form the Opo river, which flows into the Sørfjord at the church of Ullensvang, dating from the Middle Ages. The Skrikjo is considered

The upper beginnings of the »smoking« waterfall Rjukande.

part of the Opo. The Opofossen demonstrates a fall height of 650m, and is the highest waterfall in Norway. Amid this impressive scenery, monks in the Middle Ages settled in Opedal, the largest farm in Hardanger, and erected a chapel in order to convert the heathens of Hardanger.

Across from the reception area at the **Lofthus campground**, we discover a *red T* marker, and follow it up the slope.

In a few spots, the course of the path is interrupted by a farm way, but otherwise, it is a serene ascent in shady wood. Finally, the *red T* leads over the panoramic **Munketreppene** (Monks' Steps). This stairway was supposedly constructed by the monks, in order to make the steep terrain negotiable for mules. The hut Munkebu on Veivatnet Lake, further up, was also named after the monks.

Soon we reach **Nosi** (900m), with a splendid view over the Sørfjord and beyond to the glacier-covered Folgefonn peninsula, and a short distance after, we find ourselves at the »thundering« **Rjukande** waterfall.

Now the terrain flattens out, and the real Vidda begins: While the *T*-marked path leaves the course of the river and follows the *Søre Nordmannsslepa*, an old pass over the Vidda, we remain on the path near the river, whose abundance of lake-like bulges invite one to rest and bathe.

At the huts on **Opesjovatnet** Lake, the path swings up in a north-eastward direction, and meets the *T*-marked *Søre Nordmannsslepa*, which we follow on the left (westward) back to the starting point.

Several bathing spots are inviting along the lake-like bulges in the Opo river on the Hardangervidda.

18 Three-day-walk to the Litlos hut

To the plant oasis Litlos on the Hardangervidda

Middalsbu – Litlos – Hellevassbu – Middalsbu

Location: Røldal, with a stave church from the 13th century, is the centre of the valley area of the same name in the community of Odda in the west Norwegian Fylke Hordaland. Access via E 134 Drammen – Hardangervidda – Røldal – Haugesund.

Starting point: DNT hut Middalsbu (850m) north-east of Røldal; turn off the E 134 above Røldal at the Hølen campground.

Walking times: Middalsbu – Litlos 7 hrs. (21km, 1000m. alt.), Litlos – Hellevassbu 5 hrs. (17km, 250m. alt.), Hellevassbu – Middalsbu 7 hrs. (15km, 250m. alt.), total time: 19 hrs. (53km circular walk).

Ascent: 1500m.

Grade: good physical condition, sure-footedness.

Huts: Middalsbu, DNT self-serviced hut (8 berths); Litlos, DNT hostel (52 beds); Hellevassbu, DNT self-serviced hut (26 berths).

Maps: TurK 100, p. Hardangervidda Vest; TK 50, p. 1414 IV Haukelisæter and 1415 III Hårteigen.

Alternative route: The tour can be shortened to a two-day walk if you turn off to the right at Brokafossen, pass a few lakes on the way to Buadalen, and walk to Hellevassbu hut. 7 hrs., 21km from Middalsbu.

This three-day walk leads on the western Hardangervidda from hut to hut, under the influence of the Sandfloeggi (1719m), the highest elevation of the Hardangervidda, adorned with residual glaciers and covered with snow, usually year-round. Our destination, the DNT hut Litlos, is one of the plant oases of the Hardangervidda.

West of the DNT hut **Middalsbu**, we follow the *T*-marked path steeply upward along the stream, and above the tree line, swerve to the left, enjoying a wide vista: In the east, one sees the fertile Trossovdalen trough valley and the Sandfloeggi with its residual glaciers, while in the south, in one of the alpine pasture valleys, once the most beautiful of the Hardangervidda, the Valldalsvatnet reservoir is visible.

Now the path descends to **Vivassvatnet** lake, and leads upwards through **Vivassdalen** valley, into which the **Brokafossen** rushes in from the right (here, one has the opportunity to shorten the route to the Hellevassbu hut). After passing the **Tyristein** stone block on the watershed, the path descends to the **Holmavatnet**, the western headwater lake of the Kenna river. Along the river, we travel downward, then reach the path from Litlos – Hellevassbu: It leads northward to the DNT hostel **Litlos** on the **Litlosvannet** in a good hour.

Turning back from Litlos to the fork in the path, we follow the *T* markers straight on in the direction of Hellevassbu, cross the Kenna over the bridge, and let the markers direct us past several small lakes and through **Buadalen** to the fork in the path on the upper Hellevassbu, and a short distance later,

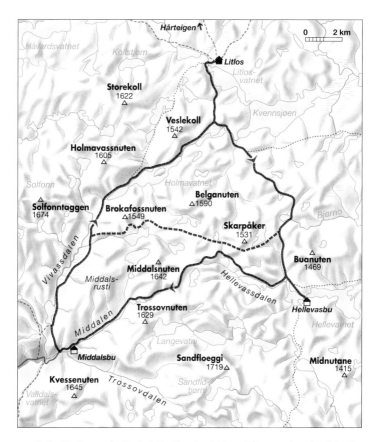

reach the **Hellevassbu Hut** at **Hedlevatnet**. From there, we turn back to the fork in the path at the upper hut, turn left, and follow the *T* markers through Middalen to the starting point, the Middalsbu hut.

East of the Middalsbu hut, the Sandfloeggi (1719m) rises up, offering a unique panorama. The ascent routes are unmarked, but the stone monument on the summit attests to the fact that the Sandfloeggi is traversed frequently. In the right weather in late summer, when there is not so much snow, you should not hesitate to view the Hårteigen once from the standpoint of this mountain.

19 To Hårteigen, 1690m

Three alternatives to the Sphinx of the Hardangervidda

Valurfossen – Hårteigen – Valurfossen

The Valurfossen.

Locations: In the west and north, Ullensvang (see walk 17), in the south and south-west, Odda (see walk 18).

Starting points: In the north, the car park at the Valurflossen (see walk 20), in the west the Lofthus campground (see walk 17), in the south the DNT hut Middalsbu (see walk 18).

Walking times: The Hårteigen cannot be walked on a one-day tour; the shortest trip there and back (north route) requires a pure walking time of approximately 18 hrs., which, depending on snow conditions (fields of old snow are still present far into the summer!), could be considerably longer.

North route, route there: Valurfossen car park – Vivell turnoff a good hour (4km, 150m. alt.), turnoff –Hedlo almost 1½ hrs. (5km, 100m. alt.), Hedlo – Hadlaskard 2½ hrs. (10km, 200m. alt.), Hadlaskard – Viersdalen – Hårteigen 4 hrs. (10km, 750m. alt.), a total time: 9–10 hrs. (29km, 1200m. alt.). For the *return route*, along the same route, approx. 9–10 hrs.

North route, return route: Hårteigen – Torehytta almost 2 hrs. (4km, no ascents, but a very steep 200m. alt. descent from the Hårteigen), Torehytta – Fagerlisete – Hedlo 6 hrs. (18km, 400m. alt.), Hedlo (– Viveli) – Valurfossen car park 3 hrs. (10km, 200m.

alt.), total time: 11 hrs. (32km, 600m. alt.).

Ascent: Valurfossen car parking – Hårteigen 1200m, *return route* via Torehytta 600m. alt.

Grade: Condition and sure-footedness, for the ascents up Hårteigen, lack of vertigo.

Huts: BT self-serviced hut Hadlaskard (1000m, 34 berths); mountain hostel Hedlo (980m), DNT hostel Litlos (1180 , 52 beds), outside of the high season, except for winter, there is self-serviced accommodation; DNT self-serviced hut Torehytta (1340m, 18 berths); mountain hostel Viveli (980m).

Variations:

West route: Lofthus – Nosi – Torehytta 12 hrs. (32km, 1600m. alt.), Torehytta – Hårteigen 2 hrs. (4km, almost 400m. alt.), total time: 14 hrs. (36km, 2000m. alt.). *Return route* 12 hrs. (36km, 300m. alt.).

If you wish to interrupt the long ascent to Torehytta, you can stay overnight in the Stavali hut (just a small distance more): Lofthus – Stavali 8 hrs. (18km, 1400m. alt.), Stavali – Torehytta 7 hrs. (17km, 500m. alt.), total time: 15 hrs. (39km, 2200m. alt.).

The steep ascent, beginning slightly above sea level, from Lofthus to Nosi, follows the route described in walk 17 over the »Monks' Steps«. As described in walk 17, we continue the walk on Nosi; we then, however, do not switch to the route along the Opo river, but rather keep to the T-marked main route, which follows the historical *Nordmannsslepa* trade route.

At both Grubbeskardvatn lakes, the path reaches an elevation of a good 1200m (excellent view). Now, the T-marked path leads downward past several small and one large lake (Kinsevatnet) to Fodnastølsvatnet (958m), at which the variation to the self-serviced Stavali hut is indicated on a sign.

Our old trade path, on the other hand, leads on to the east, ascending again, and passes more lakes in a countryside isolated from the rest of the world. We pass the mountain pasture Helnaberg, and after passing more lakes, reach the path turnoff to Torehytta.

Here, we turn off to the right and walk past the Homavatnet and southwards over the Båtadalen, then the *T*-marked route swerves to the south-east, and reaches a further panoramic area on the Kinsehøgdene, where the Hårteigen, too, stands before us in all its glory. From the Kinsehøgdene, we descend to the Torehytta (1340m).

South route: Middalsbu – Litlos 7 hrs. (21km, 1000m. alt.), Litlos – Hårteigen almost 5 hrs. (13km, 700m. alt.), total time: 11–12 hrs. (34km, 1700m. alt.). Return route 10–11 hrs. (34km, 2000m. alt.).

The walk from the Middalsu hut to Hårteigen follows the route described in walk 18 up to the Litlos hut.

From Litlos, famous for its wealth of plant life, a *T*-marked mountain path leads on through scree and residual snow to Hårteigen.

Maps: TurK 100, p. Hardangervidda Vest; TK 50, p. 1415 III Hårteigen; additionally for **1)** 1415 IV Eidfjord; for **2)** 1414 IV Haukelisæter and 1314 I Røldal; for **3)** 1315 I Ullensvang (1315 II Ringedalsvatnet is not needed).

The legendary Hårteigen is the most prominent peak of the Hardangervidda: the grey granite colossus rises up, as steep as a wall, on the western Vidda, towering over the surrounding plateau by several hundred metres. Paths lead to this »grey guide« (hárr = grey, teigen = to guide) from all directions, which is visible from most parts of the Vidda. Climbing aids enable hikers, too, to ascend. The summit of this hard mass offers a grand panorama of the Vidda and beyond to Gausta in the south-west, to the Folgefonn glacier in the west, the Hardangerjøkulen and to the Hallingskarvet in the north-east.

The steep ascent does follow a glacial mountain path through a crevasse in the eastern wall, but it is possible for snow to remain here year-round, and in the case of »hard« old snow, several close-call accidents have been reported: Extreme caution is required for the ascent, and if hard old snow is present, we recommend aborting the ascent. Instead, you can lay your ear to the western wall of the Hårteigen and hear the heart of the »Sphinx of the Hardangervidda« beating, so it is said.

Even without climbing up the mountain, the Hårteigen walk is an unforgettable experience, not least of all because one is underway for several days and nights: from hut to hut, or with a tent.

The northern access, which is presented in detail below, is the shortest, easiest, and by far the most comfortable, since – unlike the western access – the 900-vertical-metre ascent onto the Vidda is not required. It presents the least grade on physical condition of all the access routes to Hårteigen. The panoramic route follows the wide valley of the river Veig upstream, famous for its wealth of bird species.

The Hårteigen walk starting from Lofthus has the most varied countryside and, of the three Hårteigen routes, poses the greatest grade on condition, since there are no accommodation opportunities on the 32-km long stretch between Lofthus and Torehytta (however, a side-trip will take you to the Stavali self-serviced hut), and since the western edge of the Hardangervidda must also be climbed.

The walk starting from the south has the highest starting point of the three routes, at the Middalsbu hut (850m); however, the long walk to the Litlos hut on the first day requires good physical condition. All routes are marked with the *red T* symbol.

North route (*route there*): From the car park at the **Valurflossen** waterfall, we follow the *T*-marked path (see walk 20) through beautiful fjell birch wood in the direction of the mountain hostel **Viveli**, which we can see after a good hour on the opposite bank of the river Veig. Here, you must decide whether to walk over to the hostel (plan on a good ½ hour for the way there and back), or continue right on in the direction of »Hedlo«.

The *T*-marked path follows the wide river Veig upstream for a while, then leaves the bank area before the first bog, and follows the tributary Fljoto upstream (roughly to the east). After crossing the Fljoto stream soon afterward shortly before the Fljotdalsseter mountain pasture, our *T*-path leads southward up into a col area, where a magnificent view of the Veig valley opens up. Accompanied by this vista, we descend to the mountain hostel **Hedlo** (980m) on the bank of the Veig.

From the Hedlo hostel, the directional signs and *T* markers lead on in the direction »Hadlaskard«. First, our trail follows the Veig river – past a bridge – further upstream, with beautiful vistas, leads around the Rjotemyrane moorlands and reaches a crossroads at the Rjoto mountain pasture. Here, we do not continue south-east in the direction of »Sandhaug«, but rather, follow the *T* markers to the south-west, up to the panoramic **Hadlarskardhalsen**

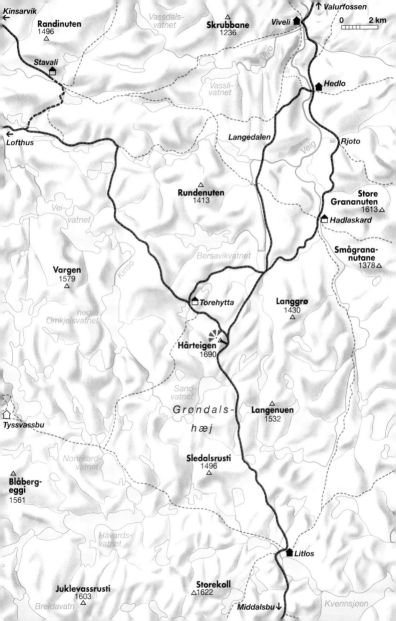

Approximately 20,000 reindeer live on the Hardangervidda.

(1133m). After a while, the path loses altitude, and descends into the Veig valley; there, shortly after passing a bridge, we reach the **Hadlaskard** hut (1000m) at the bank of the river, our next destination.

Up to the Hadlaskard hut, our walk demonstrates no problem areas. However, starting with the last sprint to the Hårteigen, we embark on a somewhat more demanding leg of the trip, along which, among other things, there may be wet areas through which we have to wade (that may pose a problem, depending on season and weather).

First we switch over to the western bank of the river at the Hadlaskard hut, over the Veig bridge, then we follow the *T* markers upstream for a short time and turn right at the next turnoff (to the south-west) down into the Kyrkjesteinsdalen. After crossing (or wading through) the stream three times in Kirchensteintal, we reach a few mountain pasture huts while following the *T* markers, and at these huts, wade through the small river Viersdøla. From the turnoff at the west bank of the river, the *T* markers lead onto the panoramic cliff **Falkabrotet** (1210m), from where we can admire the Hårteigen in all its splendour.

After descending from the Falkabrotet, the markers lead along the slope of the Smøygsdal further upwards, pass the **Torehytta path turnoff** and reach the turnoff at which the ascent to **Hårteigen** (1690m) begins.

North route (*return route*): Taking a different route back is not only recommended due to variety, but also comfort: If you select the same route as the way up at the north-eastern foot of the Hårteigen, you will have three additional hours and a spot to wade through. On the other hand, only in the north-west of the Hårteigen, at the DNT self-serviced hut **Torehytta** (1340m), located on the Øvre Solvatnet (»Upper Sun Lake«), can we reach the panoramic *T* path in only a good hour (almost 2 hrs. from the Hårteigen summit) with dry feet.

In return, two wading spots await us the next day, as well as a fairly long walk (which can be shortened through connection paths, designated on signs, to Hadlaskard): From Torehytta, we follow the *T* markers roughly to the north-east, in the direction of the noticeably towering Solnuten (1462m), switch onto the eastern slope of this mountain, covered in lush vegetation, let ourselves be guided by the markers in an easterly direction down to the Sanhaugo river, wade across it, walk on for a short time to the east, but after passing the mountain pasture huts, turn off from the trail and walk straight ahead (northward), staying in the valley of the Viersdøla (later Albogo or Olbogo).

The path follows the eastern Olbogo bank to a bridge at which a connection path branches off to Hadlaskard; via the bridge, the mountain pasture huts in Fagerlisete could be reached; however, we continue straight on (to the north), traverse a panoramic hill, cross the Olbogo river at a bridge, and follow the *T* markers through Langedalen up to a crossroads (about 1150m) on the Nuhaugane heights. There, we turn right (north-east), and, a short distance later, see the familiar destination of this leg, the **Hedlo** hut on the eastern shore of the Veig.

On the following morning, we cross the Veig again, but now branch off diagonally to the right (downstream) and, after a short, panoramic intermediate ascent, arrive at the bank of the Veo river: if we were to head straight on and cross the Veo bridge, we would arrive at the Viveli hostel.

We turn right, cross the Veig bridge and are on the familiar route again which leads us to the left (northwards, downstream) back to the starting point.

20 To the Valurfossen waterfall

Naturally beautiful walk on the north-west edge of the Hardangervidda

Car park – Valurfossen – Viveli – Skrubbhamrane – car park

Location: Community of Ullensvang, see walk 17, and Eidfjord.
Starting point: Car park (800m) above the Åsen Cafe at the end of the serpentine cul-de-sac, which branches off of Rikvei 7 Eidfjord – Geilo in Sæbø in the direction of Hjølmo.
A path also begins at Åsen Cafe to Viveli and the Valurfossen.
Walking times: Car park – Viveli, a good

hour (4km), or 2 hrs. including a side trip to the Valurfossen (9km), Viveli – Skrubbhamrane 1½ hrs. (4km), Skrubbhamrane – car park almost 2 hrs. (5km), total time: almost 5 or 6 hrs. (13 or 18km).
Ascent: 500m.
Grade: Sure-footedness.
Hut: Mountain hostel Viveli.
Maps: TurK 100, p. Hardangervidda Vest; TK 50, p. 1415 IV Eidfjord.

This walk, parts of which are very panoramic, over the fertile, lush north-west of the Hardangervidda, leads to the Valurfossen and the Viveli hostel on the border of the national park.

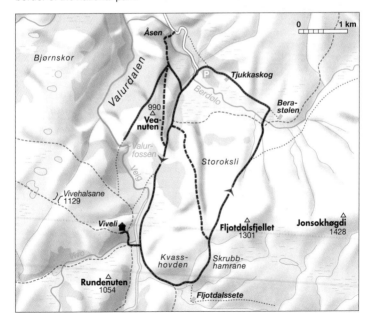

The path to Viveli repeatedly leads through idyllic fjell birch wood.

From the car park, we walk to the **Berdølo** river, cross it on the fixed bridge, and follow the »Viveli« sign on the *T*-marked path in a gentle ascent through sparse fjell birch woods. Soon, our access path merges with the old main hiking trail Eidfjord – Viveli.

If you go to the right here towards Eidfjord, you have the opportunity below to descend to the best **Valurfossen** vista point: The River Veig surmounts 272m in elevation, 67m of which in a vertical fall. The word »ur« (scree) refers to the scree at the foot of the waterfall, the word »val« stems from the old word for falcon, but also for place of death (»val-kyren«).

But our path, too, which leads upward, offers a magnificent view, and on the first treeless hilltop, we can see the protruding tip of the Hårteigen. Descending from the hilltop, we can see the **Viveli** hostel building (980 m) on the other side of the river.

Those wishing to stay there overnight cross the Veig river shortly thereafter, and then the Veo river on fixed bridges.

Returning from Viveli, we follow the Veig river further upstream, until the *T*-marked path leaves the bank area before a bog, and then follows the Fljoto tributary upstream. Shortly before the Fljotdalsseter mountain pasture, we reach a branch in the path, which would lead south to the self-serviced hut Hedlo.

Here, we begin our return trip, turn to the left and climb the steep and panoramic path up to the **Skrubbhamrane**, where we reach yet another turnoff in the path. Here, we keep diagonally to the right and walk on the slope of the **Fljotdalsfjellet** with a magnificent view back on the Berdølo river. After crossing the bridge, we go left, back to the starting point.

21 Over the northeast of the Hardangervidda

Three-day walk over the eastern Hardangervidda

Halne – Heinseter – Rauhellern – Halne

Location: The community Hol in the Fylke Buskerud encompasses the north-east of the Hardangervidda, as well as the greater portion of the mountain ridge Hallingskarvet; the most well-known town is the winter sport centre of Geilo (see walk 22).
Starting point: Ships' landing at Halnefjorden (1130m) near the mountain hostel Halne on Riksvei 7 Geilo – Eidfjorden. The water taxis run in the summer main season, and the crossing takes 45 minutes. Generally, there are two boats leaving per day, one in the morning and one in the afternoon. The exact schedule is posted at the landing.
Walking times: Sleipa – Heinseter 2 hrs. (6km, 150m. alt.), Heinseter – Rauhellern 4 hrs. (14km, 200m. alt.), Rauhellern – Sleipa 4 hrs. (14km, 150m. alt.), total time: 10 hrs. (34km).

Ascent: 500m.
Grade: Good physical condition and sure-footedness.
Huts: Heinseter, privately-managed mountain hostel (40 beds, discount for DNT members); Rauhellern, staffed DOT hostel (58 beds) plus, outside of the season, an open extension with 4 berths; Stigstuv, privately-managed hostel (30 beds), in the off-season, 9 berths on a self-catering basis are available.
Maps: TurK 100, p. Hardangervidda Øst; TK 50, p. 1415 I Bjoreio and 1515 IV Hein.
Alternative route: If you want to remain independent of the boat schedule, starting from the Rauhellern hostel, follow the *T* markers to the Stigstuv hostel (4 hrs., 14km) and, from Stigstuv, return to Halne on the *T*-marked path (5 hrs., 16km).

After a boat ride across the interior lake Halnefjorden, this three-day walk, on which there are hardly any ascents, leads through the north-eastern portion of the Hardangervidda National Park. The lake is situated outside of the national park, whereas Heinseter and Rauhellern lie within the conservation area.

From the ships' landing at the **Sleipa** reservoir, we follow the *red T* markers up a gentle slope eastwards with a spectacular view of the Halnefjorden and beyond to the Hardangerjøkulen glacier and of the Øvre Hein lake and beyond to the Hallingskarvet massif. After crossing the **Selstjørnutan** hills, the trail descends to the **Heinseter** hostel (1098m) on the river Heinelvi.

From Heinseter, the *T* markers lead onto the eastern incline of the **Selstjørnutan**; after crossing the stream flowing from the Selstjørni lakes, we traverse the panoramic **Geitsjøhovda** and reach the *Nordmannsslepa*, one of the historical Hardangervidda trails, in the **Djupa** valley; this old trail connected the east and the west of the Vidda. We follow it a short distance upstream in the Djupa valley. Then, *T* markers point out the further route in the valley to the DOT hostel **Rauhellern** (1221m) on Langesjøen lake.

The *T* markers leave the hostel and go up in a northerly direction. Before the summit plateau of the **Langsjønutan** mountains, the path swerves diagonally to the left in a north-westerly direction, and then reaches a turnoff in the path. Whereas the turnoff to the left leads to the Stigstuv hostel (11 more km), we walk straight on in the direction of »Halne«. At the next turnoff, we turn right (north); the way to Halne continues straight on (another 20km).

We cross the *Nordmannsslepa*, discernible as a path, and reach the wide, high-lying valley **Skyttarbudalen**, and once again arrive at the **Halnefjorden**. We follow its shoreline back to the ships' landing.

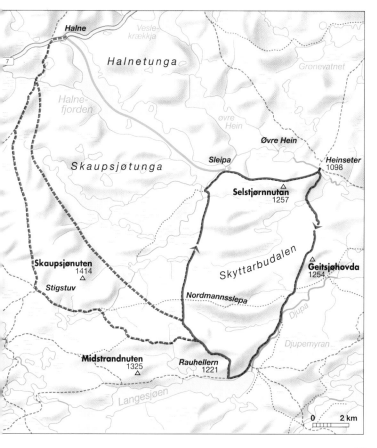

22 Prestholtskarvet, 1863m

Panoramic tour on the Hallingskarvet

Prestholtseter – Prestholtskarvet – Prestholtseter

Location: Geilo (pop. 2500) in Ustedalen, at the foot of the mountain chain Hallingskarvet, is the most significant winter sport location in Scandinavia, and one of the most important active-holiday centres in Norway, with its corresponding offer of skiing, hiking, fishing and general outdoor supply shops, several hotels and campgrounds, as well as chair-lifts and T-bars, a railway, ski schools, etc. Via cableway, the panoramic Geilohøgda (1100m) can be reached from the town. Geilo is situated in the community of Hol, in the south-eastern Norwegian Fylke Bus-kerud.

Starting point: Car park at the Prestholtseter mountain pasture (1250m), west-northwest of Geilo.

Walking times: Prestholtseter – Prestholtskarvet a good 3 hrs., descent 3 hrs., total time: 6 hrs. (11km).

Ascent: 600m.

Grade: Good physical condition, sure-footedness in steep scree and rocky terrain.

Maps: Cappelens Kart 1:100,000, p. Skarvheimen; TurK 100, p. Hardangervidda Øst; TK 50, p. 1516 III Hallingskarvet.

This partially very steep walk with spectacular views leads through the Prestholtskarvet on the eastern part of the long Hallingskarvet mountain ridge. The Prestholtskarvet is one of the few, but very remarkable, wind gaps in a steep precipice, in places as sheer as a wall, with which the mountain ridge falls away in the summit area down to the Ustedalen valley. The name Prestholtskarvet (Priests' Wood Gap) may conjure up false images: There

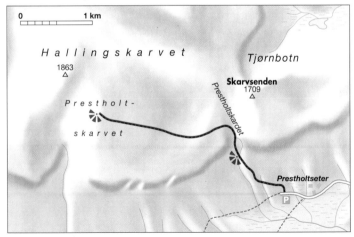

View of Geilo and beyond to the Prestholskarvet.

are no »woods« here, or any trees for that matter; there is all the more ice and snow, which usually remains year round.

From the huts on the **Prestholtseter** mountain pasture (1260m), in a location with a spectacular outlook, the directional sign »Prestholtskarvet« and a few *red T* markers lead up a steep and panoramic path, crossing the mountain slope in the ascent, with a view to the south over the Ustedalen valley and beyond to the east of the Hardangervidda.

The crossing ascent soon turns into a scree-covered ascent in the fall line, whereby the deeply cut Prestholtskarvet, the »Priests' Wood Gap«, is the destination. In the eternal snow of the gorge-like notch, our markers soon switch over to the valley flank towering up in the west, and lead up a constant incline, somewhat less steep. Soon, the terrain begins to flatten out, and the panoramic final sprint on the high ridge of the Hallingskarvet to the **Prestholtskarvet** heights (1863m) begins.

The view sweeps over Lake Ustevatnet in Ustedalen, to the Hardangervidda. On the other side of this plateau, one can see Gausta when visibility is clear, and on the plateau, even from the south-west, the Hårteigen is visible as the highest elevation, and in the west, the white-blue of the Hardangerjøkulen glacier can be seen. In the south-east, the houses of the winter sport centre Geilo come into view.

The descent is made on the same route as the ascent.

23 Sankt Pål, 1694 m

Panoramic summit opposite the Hardangerjøkulen glacier

Finse – Klemsbu – Sankt Pål – Finse

Location: The winter sport centre Finse is situated in the community of Ulvik in the western Norwegian Fylke Hordaland, on the Finsevatnet between the Hardangerjøkulen glacier and the Hallingskarvet mountain ridge. Finse has no public street access, but it does have Norway's highest train station (1222m) on the Bergen rail line. In Finse, the »Snow Capital«, an absence of snow can only be expected during a few weeks of high summer; on the other hand, the ski conditions are good most of the year.

Starting point: Finsehytta (1222m) on the railway line »Bergensbanen« Oslo – Høne-foss – Gol – Geilo – Flåm – Bergen. Car access via Riksvei 7, Geilo – Eidfjorden to Haugastøl, to the train station (»stasjon«) of the Bergen railway.

Walking times: Finse – Sankt Pål, 2 hrs., return route 2 hrs., total time: 4 hrs. (13km).

Ascent: 500m.

Grade: Sure-footedness in terrain which is covered with scree and often snow.

Hut: Finsehytta, DNT mountain hotel (150 beds).

Maps: Cappelens Kart 1:100,000, p. Skarvheimen; TK 50, p. 1416 II Hardanger-jøkulen.

Tip: The Finsehytta is the base camp for the DNT glacier course. Hikers are warned not to go on the Hardangerjøkulen glacier without an experienced guide, which has been subject to strong dynamic forces in recent years.

Biking tip: The road from Haugastøl – Finse – Flåm (80km), built during the construction of the Bergen railway high-mountain expanse, the Rallarvegen, closed to public traffic, is one of the best-known mountain bike routes in Norway. From Haugastøl (990m) to Finse (1222m), you travel 27km on the Rallarvegen.

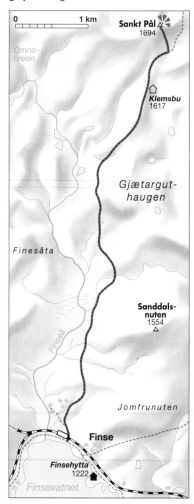

On the Rallarvegen.

This walk leads from the car-free winter sport centre of Finse on a route with unique views of the Hardangerjøkulen and Hardangervidda to Sankt Pål. The area, experiencing a great deal of precipitation, is a water conservation area: camping is forbidden.

From the **Finsehytta**, we follow the *red T* markers to the Finse railway station, cross the tracks and walk upwards between huts, and then on the path in the valley of the Finseåa, which offers a captivating view over Finse and beyond the Finsevatnet to the Hardangerjøkulen, which, at 78km^2, is the fifth-largest glacier in Norway.

Since the Bergen railway was opened (1909), the Hardangerjøkulen plateau glacier has been one of the most significant sights in Norway; the DNT offers glacier courses on the Hardangerjøkulen.

After crossing the Finseåa on a bridge, the *T* markers in this arctic area, in which fields of snow can endure year-round, lead upward. We pass the **Klemsbu** (1617m), a storm shelter, and a short distance later can enjoy the splendid panorama on **Sankt Pål** (1694m): In the south, the Hardangerjøkulen is visible in all its glory, in the south-east of the Hardangervidda, the mighty dome of the Gaustatoppen rises up, and in the north-east, the Hurrungane peaks in the west of Jotunheimen are visible.

The name of the round, dome-like Sankt Pål traces back to the English hunter and fisher Lord Garvagh, who, in 1860, was in the area for reindeer hunting, and, upon seeing the mountain, was reminded of Saint Paul's Cathedral in London.

24 To Fannaråken, 2068m

Panoramic tour between Hurrungane and Jotunheimen

Turtagrø – Helgedalen – Fannaråkhytta – Keisarpasset – Turtagrø

Starting point: Turtagrø mountain hotel (884m) on Riksvei 55 Sognefjord – Sognefjell – Jotunheimen – Lom; the national road through the Sognefjell (Sognefjellvegen) is closed in winter.

Walking times: Turtagrø – Fannaråkhytta 4 hrs., Fannaråkhytta – Keisarpasset a good hour, Keisarpasset – Turtagrø 2 hrs., total time: 7 hrs. (17km circular walk).

Ascent: 1200m.

Grade: Knowledge of the weather; sure-footedness in terrain which is partially very steep and full of scree and rock, and which can be covered in snow year-round in spots.

Huts: Mountain hotel Turtagrø (80 beds); Fannaråkhytta, DNT self-serviced hut (35 berths), closed in winter.

Maps: TurK 100, p. Jotunheimen; TK 50, p. 1518 III Sygnefjell and 1517 IV Hurrungane.

This very steep panoramic walk leads over a well-developed mountain path onto the very panoramic Fannaråken, the glacial mountain ridge (fanna = fonni = firn, råken = ridge) between the peaks of Jotunheimen and Hurrungane.

The northern side is covered by glacier, while our marked route leads over the glacier-free western ridge, which, however, can be covered with snow well into the summer. There is the opportunity for accommodation in Fannaråkhytta, the highest overnight hut in Scandinavia.

The hut is the destination of guided glacier tours from the north-east. Starting from the Sognefjellhytta and Krossbu hostels – both located in the north-east of the Fannaråken in the Sognefjell – daily tours are offered in the high season to the Fannaråken via the Fannaråkbreen glacier (register on the evening before the tour). You should dress warmly for the tour and be prepared for sudden changes in weather; the average temperature on the Fannaråken in July is 2.5°C.

The view spans over the Syngefjell to Fannaråken and to the Hurrungane towering in the background.

From the **Turtagrø** mountain hotel, we follow National Road 55 for about 5 minutes upwards, until, at a left curve, a trail branches off to the right into **Helgedalen**. A short time later, it merges into a road closed to public traffic, which leads further into the valley, to the entrance of the water draw-off tunnel (for the power plant in Fortun). At the turnoff, our *T* markers lead up to the left, and from there into the national park, left unspoilt by the power plant industry, and reach, via steep serpentines, the path turnoff to which we will come on the descent from the right (east).

The ascent route leads further up into the **Steindalen** along serpentines. At **Ekrehytta**, we traverse the border to the national park. A short distance later, the mountain path swerves onto the panoramic **Fannaråken** west ridge, on which we reach the **Fannaråkhytta** (2068m): The view stretches from the north and north-east over the Fannaråkbreen and beyond to the Sognefjell and Jotunheimen, while in the south, the glacial battlement of the Hurrungane climbing region rises up.

From the Fannaråkhytta, we follow the *T* markers eastward to the **Fannaråknosa** and down a panoramic stretch to the **Keisarpasset** turnoff; below lies Skogadalen, and the Skogadalsbøen staffed hut, to which the *T* markers lead straight on; however, we turn off to the right at the Emperor's Pass, and follow the *T* markers back to **Steindalen**.

25 To Skåla, 1843m

Strenuous panoramic walk between Nordfjord and Jostedalsbreen

Loen – Skåla – Loen

Location: The community of Stryn lies in the western Norwegian Fylke Sogn og Fjordane on the inner Nordfjord and the Jostedalsbreen.
Access via Riksvei 60 Byrkjelo – Stryn – Stranda (– Ålesund).
Starting point: Car park charging a fee (20m) east of Loen at Tyva.
Walking times: Loen – Skåla 5 hrs., return route 3 hrs., total time: 8 hrs. (14km). Side trip to the Vesleskåla almost 1 hour (100m. alt.) more.

Ascent: 1800m.
Grade: Good physical condition, sure-footedness in steep terrain with rocks and scree, which, in upper elevations, is mostly covered with snow.
Hut: Skålatårnet, BT self-serviced hut (10 berths); in and around Loen, whose centre is the white church with the stone cross, there are several campgrounds and the exclusive Hotel Alexandra.
Maps: TurK 100, p. Jostedalsbreen; TK 50, p. 1318 I Stryn and 1418 IV Lodalskåpa.

From Loen on the inner Nordfjord, this panoramic walk leads steeply up to the summit of the Skåla, which offers an unsurpassed vista of the Jostedalsbreen and the fjords and summits in the western Norwegian Sogn og Fjordane. With 1800 metres of altitude of ascent, this is one of the »highest« walks in Norway. Since the starting point is located at approximately sea level, the trail leads through all vegetation zones and terrain – from wood to scree, from meadows and mountain pastures to ice and snow-covered, steep escarpments. The path is well tended; however, further up, the steps may partially be covered with snow, even in high summer.

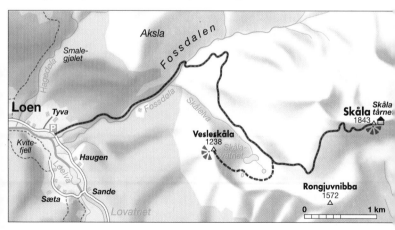

Above Loen, view of Skåla.

The mountain path was established from 1905–1914, for health-related reasons: hiking on the Skåla was supposed to primarily prevent lung disease. The name skåla (bowl) refers to the fact that the prominent, striking col of the mountain massif looks like a bowl.

From the car park at Tjugen = **Tyva** at the river Loelva, we follow the *red T* markers next to a tributary of the Fossdøla stream upwards. The path leads steeply upwards in the wooded, partly deeply-carved valley of the Fossdøla, which cascades over rocks.

Above the tree line, we cross the Fossdøla on a bridge, and walk on a panoramic stretch through mountain pasture meadow towards the **Skåla-vatnet** (1142m), and the terrain becomes strewn with scree. When visibility is clear, we recommend the side trip from the lake to the **Vesleskåla** (1238m); it offers a magnificent view (better than the one from the Skåla) of the Nordfjord and its surroundings.

At the lake, the steep descent, partially made more negotiable by steps, to the col between Skåla and Sandsnibba, followed by another steep ascent over rock and scree and, usually, snow or ice. Once the terrain begins to flatten out, we can expect the final ascent, lined with slabs, to the ridges of the **Skåla** (1843m), plunging vertically to the north and south.

The **Skålatårnet** (Skåla Tower), which functions as a self-serviced hut on the summit, is a two-storey tower with 1.5-m thick walls erected in 1891 in a private initiative.

26 To the ice-covered Glittertind, 2464m

Two-day walk over the »Glitter Battlement« in Jotunheimen

Spiterstulen – Glittertind – Glitterheim – Spiterstulen

Location: The Tourist Centre Lom in the Fylke Oppland is a suburb of the mountain community of the same name in Jotunheimen, on both sides of Ottadalen, a secondary valley to the right of the Gudbrandsdalen. The church, which today serves as a reformed parish church, is one of the few stave churches (from about 1190), on which parts of the medieval roof ridge, with an original dragon's head, are still in existence. In Garmostræe, near Garmo, Knut Hamsun was born in 1859 (museum monument).

Starting point: Mountain hotel Spiterstulen (1106m) in Visdalen south-west of Lom at the end of a toll road which branches off of Riksvei 55.

Walking times: Spiterstulen – Glittertind 4 hrs., Glittertind – Glitterheim almost 3 hrs., Glitterheim – Spiterstulen 7 hrs., total time 14 hrs. (31 km).

Ascent: 1700m.

Grade: Good physical condition, sure-footedness and a good sense of orientation. At the starting point, find out whether the ice cap of the Glittertind can be traversed without crampons (usually it can).

Huts: Mountain hotel Spiterstulen (DNT discount; there is a small area to pitch a tent next to it); DNT mountain hotel Glitterheim (130 beds, no cars, only accessible on foot or with a bicycle).

Maps: TurK 100, p. Jotunheimen; TK 50, p. 1518 II Galdhøpiggen and 1618 III Glittertinden.

A look back at the ice cap of the Glittertind during the descent to Glitterheim.

From the Glittertind, the view falls on Galdhøpiggen (on right, with the distinct »gate«), and on the horizon, the Hurrungane battlement.

The Glittertind, with its unmistakable snow cornice cap, was the highest peak in Scandinavia until the 1980's, when the crown was passed on to the neighbouring Galdhøpiggen. The measurement taken in 1931 noted the highest point of the Glittertind at 2481m; in the following decades, the ice melted down to 2472m (1978), and since 1984, its height is noted at 2464m. The Galdhøpiggen, on the other hand, reaches 2469m, and is thus higher than the Glittertind, whether with or without (2452m) the ice cap. However, the Glittertind is definitely a magnificent destination. We incorporate the ascent routes from Spiterstulen and Glitterheim into a two-day mountain walk which leaves no wishes unfulfilled with regard to the wealth of vistas and the quality of the experience. The *T*-marked route passes through large boulder terrain; in the presence of smooth ice, crampons may be required.

From the mountain hotel **Spiterstulen**, we follow the toll road a short way upward, until the *red T* markers switch over to the steep escarpment. After a long, steep ascent, the panoramic terrain flattens out in the col between Skautkampen and Skauthø, and we reach a turnoff in the path. Straight ahead (diagonally to the right), the path leads in the direction of Glitterheim (our return route), while we turn off to the left in the direction of Glittertind, crossing a brook, and then the wider stream Skauta over stepping stones, and finally climb up the deeply-cut valley of the Steindalshelva stream in the eastern flank of the Glittertind. The boulder and scree-strewn terrain, which becomes ever steeper, requires the occasional use of your hands. Then, we reach the ice-covered summit of the **Glittertind** (approx. 2464m). Do not stray too far to the north, because there is a dangerous cornice! An extravagant panorama entices the hiker to linger; to the north, you can make out the Trollsteinseggi ridge between glaciers. To date, all shelters erected on the summit ice have fallen victim to stormy weather, the last in 1978. From the summit, we keep to the south for a short (!) time, then turn to the east (i.e. do not follow the broken-away edge), where we once again find *T* markers on

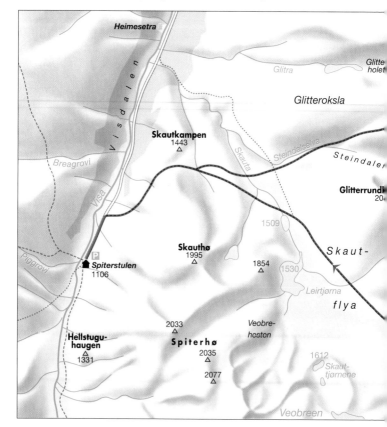

the edge of the ice field. The markers lead through terrain which is panoramic and, at the beginning, strewn with large boulders, and on to the DNT mountain hotel **Glitterheim** in the valley of the glacial river Veo. From Glitterheim, the *red T* markers lead upwards through the bizarre Veodalen, characterised by ice. Shortly before the river exits the Veobreen glacier, the markers lead up to the right in the **Vesleglupen** gorge (which in winter poses an avalanche risk), passes the usually frozen **Veslegluptjørnene** lakes, and then passes through the stony **Skautflya** plateau. Finally, we reach the Glittertind ascent route once again, and walk it back to **Spiterstulen**.

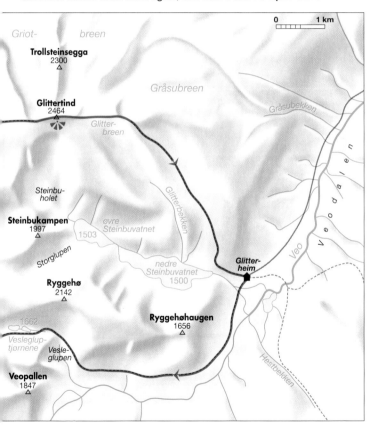

27 Galdhøpiggen, 2469m

To the highest summit in northern Europe

Spiterstulen – Galdhøpiggen – Spiterstulen

Location: Lom, see walk 26.
Starting point: Mountain hotel Spiterstulen (1106m) in Visdalen, south-west of Lom at the end of a toll road which branches off from Riksvei 55.
Walking times: Spiterstulen – Galdhøpiggen 4 hrs., descent 2 hrs., total time 6 hrs. (11km).
Ascent: 1400m.
Grade: Knowledge of weather, sure-footedness in steep, partially exposed scree and boulder terrain which, in parts, is covered by snow on a year-round basis.
Huts: Mountain hotel Spiterstulen (DNT discount; there is a small area to pitch a tent next to it); shelter (not overnight accommodation) on Galdhøpiggen (wool blankets, small stove, tea bags, bucket with (frozen) water); normally, the hut is open when the glacier guide is present; then, one does pay the caretaker for provisions taken inde-

pendently. There is no regular accommodation possibility.
Maps: TurK 100, p. Jotunheimen; TK 50, p. 1518 II Galdhøpiggen.
Alternative route: Hikers having experience in and equipment for glacier hiking start in the early summer three hours before sunrise at the mountain hostel Juvvasshytta and take the route over the Styggebreen (5km, 650m. alt.), whereby the finale on the rocky ridge is partially steep and exposed. From Galdhøpiggen, the descent follows the normal route to the mountain hotel Spiterstulen. From there, take the marked route via the permafrost plateau of the Juvflya back to the Juvvasshytta. The total length of this circular walk, which is excellent, although you do have to carry your glacier equipment, that you only actually need for a few kilometres, around with you the whole time: 8 hrs., 17km and 1400m. alt. for the ascent.

View from Galdhøpiggen to the Hurrungane and Fannaråk massif.

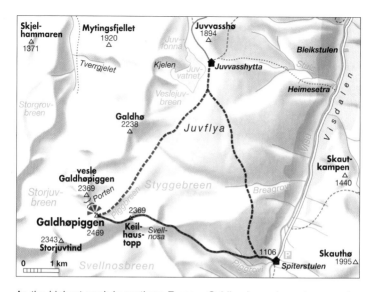

As the highest peak in northern Europe, Galdhøpiggen is such a popular destination that we recommend not climbing it on a sunny holiday weekend. The recommended normal route follows a *T*-marked, panoramic high-mountain path typical for Norway, partially strewn with large rocks and scree, residual snow, subject to quick changes in weather, etc. Thus, the appropriate mountain equipment is essential.

The starting point is the mountain hotel **Spiterstulen**. It evolved from an alpine farm, which was first used for mountain-climbing accommodation as early as 1836; a few huts are over 200 years old. Below the mountain hotel, the *red T* markers lead onto a bridge over the Visa stream, then steeply upwards, passing the Juvvassytta turnoff. The ascent leads further steeply up the panoramic slope, before the terrain begins to flatten out after almost two hours, and we reach the preliminary peak, the **Svellnosi** (2272m) on the edge of the glacier. The **Keilhaus topp** summit (2355), which we reach a short distance later, is named after the Jotunheimer »discoverer« and geologist Balthasar Mathias Keilhau, who broke off an attempt to be the first to reach the Galdhøpiggen summit in 1844 due to a change in the weather (the first known successful ascent of the Galdhøpiggen summit was in 1850, by Steinar Sulheim, J. Flaaten and J. Arnesen). Now, the final ascent, strewn with scree, ice and snow, to **Galdhøpiggen** (2469m) begins, on which a tremendous panorama, stretching all the way to the ocean, opens up.

28 To Kyrkja, 2032m

To the church of rock, Kyrkja in Jotunheimen

Leirvassbu – Kyrkja – Leirvassbu

Location: Lom, see walk 26.
Starting point: Leirvassbu hostel (1405m), south-south-west of Lom at the end of a toll road which branches off from Riksvei 55.
Walking times: Leirvassbu – Kyrkja a good 2 hrs., return route 2 hrs., total time 4 hrs. (9km).
Ascent: 650m.

Grade: A good sense of orientation, knowledge of the weather, sure-footedness and a lack of vertigo in steep rock and boulder terrain which is partially exposed and requires the use of your hands.
Hut: Leirvassbu hostel (140 beds).
Maps: TurK 100, p. Jotunheimen; TK 50, p. 1518 ll Galdhøpiggen.

This mostly unmarked or sparsely marked walk, due to rock piles, leads through boulders in partially blocked-off terrain to the panoramic summit of the Kyrkja, surrounded by lakes. The name of the mountain comes from the fact that, separated by its »church-tower like« shape, it towers above the other mountains in the area from the converging valleys. At the end of the 19th century, it was still considered insurmountable, a concept which is understandable when the mountain is observed from its north side (where the *T*-marked route from Leirvassbu – Spiterstulen runs).
From the **Leirvassbu** hostel, we follow the road, closed to public traffic, above the **Leirvatnet** gently uphill, accompanied by a lovely view of the profile of Kyrkja. At the point where the path swerves to the right, we branch

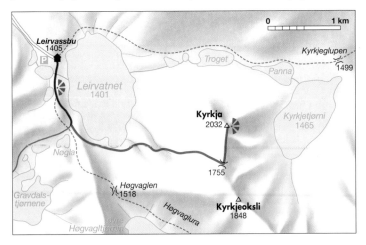

During the approach, the Tvenbotntindane come into view beyond the Leirvatnet.

off to the left, towards the lake shore, follow the shoreline area, and then climb steeply up to the col (1755m) between Kyrkjeoksli and Kyrkja. Now we head to the left (northward) onto the steep, rocky ridge to the summit of **Kyrkja** (2032m).

29 Over the Besseggen ridge

Over the »Scythe Ridge« Besseggen in Jotunheimen

Gjendesheim – Besseggen – Memurubu – Gjendesheim

A side view of the Besseggen ridge as seen from Bessvatnet.

The Besseggen ridge, between the Bessvatnet and Gjende lakes, is the classic walk in Norway. It offers a fascinating view of both lakes, as well as the summit and glacier of Jotunheimen. A short stretch of the trail may be considered exposed, but otherwise, this is a normal high-mountain ascent with scree, rocks, sun and fields of snow.

From the DNT hut **Gjendesheim**, we follow the *red T* markers upwards (northward) along the slope of **Gjendeshalsen**, then turn off at the Glitterheim turnoff diagonally to the left, and, after crossing the small **Veltløyfti** gorge, reach the treeless, panoramic plateau of the **Veslefjellet**.

On the Veslefjell (1743m), from which a mighty stone monument towers, the sunny stretch of the walk begins, with a marvellous view to the west and many spots in which to linger. Shortly after traversing the summit, the precisely-marked route reaches the Besseggen and follows the ridge steeply

Location: Vågåmo is the centre of the community of Vågå, which encompasses the north-eastern Jotunheimen, an diverse area. The settlement was constructed around the stave church (Vågå kirke) at the mouth of the Finna and Otta rivers.

Starting point: DNT mountain hotel Gjendessheim (995m) south of Vågåmo on Riksvei 51; bus line Otta – Gol.

Walking times: Gjendesheim – Memurubu a good 6 hrs., return route along the shore almost 4 hrs., total time 10 hrs. (22km).

Ascent: 1100m.

Grade: Sure-footedness, and in a few places, a lack of vertigo.

Huts: DNT mountain hotel Gjendesheim (143 beds); mountain inn Memurubu (owned by the DNT, 140 beds).

Maps: TurK 100, p. Jotunheimen; TK 50 (not very handy), p. 1617 IV Gjende and 1618 III Glittertinden.

Alternative route: It is definitely worth it to continue hiking from Memurubu on to the DNT hut Gjendebu on the western bay of the lake (see walk 30).

Boat traffic: The walk can be shortened by a good 3 hrs. if the return route is made from Memurubu to Gjendesheim by boat (luggage can be transported). In the summer, from the beginning of July to the end of August, the ship »MS Gjende« travels between Gjendesheim, Memurubu and Gjendebu; Gjendesheim – Memurubu 35 min.; Memurubu – Gjendebu as well. In Gjendesheim, the boat runs daily at 7:00 a.m., 9:55 a.m. (only to Memuburu) and 11:30 a.m., as well as Fridays additionally at 4:00 p.m.; these departure times are subject to change. If you plan on taking the boat from Memurubu to Gjendesheim after the Besseggen walk, you must definitely look at the current schedule before beginning the walk, in order to avoid any rude awakenings in Memuburu. In an emergency, you can purchase anything you need for an unplanned overnight accommodation, including a toothbrush, at exceedingly expensive prices, at the Memuruburu hostel.

View of Bessvatnet and beyond to the Nautgardstinden massif.

downward to **Bandet**, the band of rocks between the **Bessvatnet** and the cliff walls dropping down to Lake Gjende – a pretty place for a rest with a view.

The Bandet descends 8m to the north down to the Bessvatnet and on the south side drops 398m to the lake. This beautiful piece of nature has been under protection since the establishment of the national park. Primarily during the descent, the various colours of both lakes become apparent: Gjende lake is emerald to milky green from the glacier water; Bessvatnet lake, on the other hand, is blue. Beyond Bessvatnet, the mighty Besshøi group rises up (2258m).

From Bandet, the *red T* markers lead up to the **Bjørnbøltjørna** lakes, where the route now moves away from the broken-off edge of Gjende lake, and is less panoramic. Soon after, the view spans the imposing U-shaped Memuru-dalen valley, and the descent to Memurubu begins.

From the Memurubu hut, the shore trail leads back to Gjendesheim. The shore trail is also a typical mountain path, but it usually meanders through fjell birch wood and the fertile vegetation for which the shore of Gjende lake is famous: the plants have a sunny spot protected from wind, and the brooks trickling down provide sufficient moisture (which is noticeable in several boggy areas), such that flowers which have become rare here have found a place to regenerate.

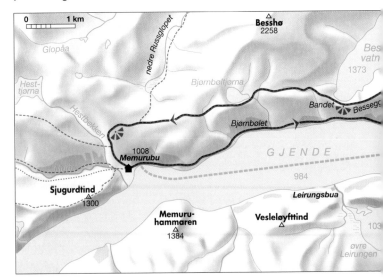

At Bessaggen, the magnificent view reaches out over Gjende lake; below, the boat sails to Gjendesheim.

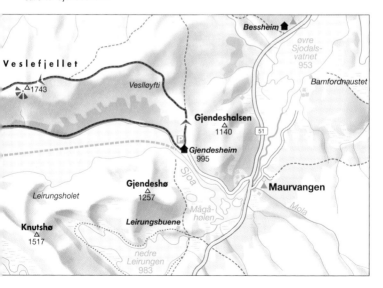

30 Over the Memurutunga

Excellent panoramic walk in Jotunheimen National Park

Memurubu – Memurutunga – Gjendebu – return trip via ship

Starting point: Memurubu (1008m), mountain inn, accessible as in walk 29 or by boat from Gjendesheim (departure times, see walk 29).

Walking times: Memurubu – stone monument 3 hrs., stone monument – Gjendebu via Bukkelægret 2 hrs., or via Storådalen 4 hrs., total time 5 hrs. / 7 hrs. (11km / 18km).

Ascent: 400m.

Grade: Sure-footedness, and in the ex-posed Bukkelægret, a lack of vertigo.

Huts: DNT mountain hotel Memurubu (140 beds); DNT hostel Gjendebu (115 beds). Due to the boat traffic, both hostels are well-visited.

Maps: TurK 100, p. Jotunheimen; TK 50, p. 1617 IV Gjende and 1618 III Glittertinden.

Alternative route: 2km after the Lågtunga, a turnoff leads to the right back to the Memurubu hostel; total time 4 hrs. and almost 580m. alt. for the round trip.

Starting from the car-free Memurubu hostel at the shore of Gjende lake, this panoramic walk over the Memurutunga, which is very steep and exposed on the Bukkelægret, leads through one of the most panoramic mountain areas of Jotunheimen. The return trip from the DNT hostel Gjendebu, also car-free, at the western shore of the lake, is made by boat (for departure times, see walk 29). The walk enjoys a high degree of popularity and is accordingly well-visited in the main season.

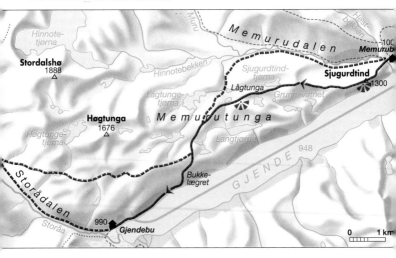

On the ascent up Memurutunga, one can see the alluvial cone which the glacial river Muru deposits as it flows into Gjende lake.

From the **Memurubu** hostel (1008m), the *red T* markers lead over a bridge crossing the Muru glacial river, and guides us steeply, constantly accompanied by a marvellous view of **Sjugurdtinden** (1300m), between Gjende lake and the U-shaped Memurudalen valley, and further up to Lake **Sjugurdtintjørnet** (1443m) on the mountain »tongue«, **Lågtunga**. On the other side of the lake, the alpine peaks of the »Gjende Alps« can be seen, while, in the north, the Memurutindane and Surtningssui rise up from glaciers. The Surtningssui is considered one of the most panoramic summits in Jotunheimen that can be reached on a trail; weather-permitting, you should not hesitate.

Two km further, we pass the turnoff (on the right) to Memurudalen valley, and follow the *T* markers further upwards to a **stone monument**. Here, the route forks: To the left, the exposed descent route leads through the **Bukkelægret**, secured in a few spots with iron clamps, railings and other holds. We descend steeply to Gjende lake, and follow the avalanche-endangered shore area through fjell birch wood on the right, to the ships' landing and **Gjendebu** hut (990m).

If you wish to circumvent the exposed descent – which we recommend if there is a lot of residual snow and ice –, take the route through **Storådalen**, which is about 2 hrs. longer.

31 Over the Skinneggen crest

Two-lake walk between Bygdin and Tyin

Eidsbugarden – Utsikten – Skinneggen – Utsikten – Tyin

Location: The mountain and winter-sport community of Vang in the eastern Norwegian Fylke Oppland encompasses the south-eastern Jotunheimen with the Bygdin and Tyin lakes, Vangsmjøsa lake, through which the Begna flows, and parts of the Fillefjell. There are many stave churches in the Vang community area, some altered (Høre), some reconstructed (Øye). The »Vinjestugu« museum in Eidsbugarden remembers the poet and hiker Aasmund Olavsson Vinje (1818–1870), who coined the name »Jotunheimen«.

Starting point: Holiday settlement Eidsbugarden (1062m) on the western shore of Bygdin lakes; access via E 16 Oslo – Fagernes – Vang to Tyinkrysset / Hugostua, then via Riksvei 53 and Riksvei 252 (in the winter, it is a cul-de-sac which is not cleared) via Tyinholmen to Eidsbugarden.

Destination point: Tyin.

Boat: The »MS Bitihorn« runs approximately from the end of June until approximately the beginning of September twice daily to Eidsbugarden, Torfinnsbu and Bygdin (accessible via Riksvei 51 Fagernes – Vågå). This boat ride, with beautiful views of the countryside, enables hikes in the Gjende Alps, i.e. in the mountain area between the Bygdin and Gjende lakes, with the Torfinnsbu hut as a starting point. Plan on a good 5 hours for the *T*-marked route from Torfinnsbu to Gjendebu.

Walking times: Eidsbugarden – Utsikten

1½ hrs. (3km., 500m. alt.), Utsikten – P1607 – Utsikten 1½ hrs. (5km., 200m. alt.), Utsikten – Tyinholmen 1 hr. (3km), total time 4 hrs. (11km).

Ascent: 700m.

Grade: Sure-footedness and a good sense of orientation.

Hut: Eidsbugarden (hotels, cafeteria, camping), Tyinholmen Høyfjellshotell.

Maps: Cappelens kart 1:100,000, p. Skarvheimen; TurK 100, p. Jotunheimen; TK 50, p. 1517 I Tyin.

From Eidsbugarden on Bygdin lake in the south of Jotunheimen, this walk leads to the panoramic spot Utsikten (»vista point«), which inspired Edvard Grieg to write his prologue »On Skinneggen« in his »Travel Memoirs of Fjell and Fjord«, op. 44, who, while on the Aasmund Olafsson Vinje, wrote the poem »Jøtunheimen«, from where the mountain range takes its name. The walk is designed as a one-way route. Make sure to be at the bus stop in

Tyinholmen on time, otherwise you will have to walk 4 extra kilometres. The departure times for the busses are posted at the starting point; they are co-ordinated with the departure times for the boats.

From the ships' landing in **Eidsbugarden**, we follow the street for a short distance inland, then turn left (south) at the first path, and walk up a path marked with *red T* markers in moderately steep terrain to **Utsikten** (1518m), the most famous vista point of the Skinneggen crest between the Bygdin and Tyin lakes (Skinneggen = crest between the lakes): to the west, the peaks of the Hjelledalstinden and Falketind rise up, as well as the Hurrungane behind them, and to the north, the view spans to Galdhøpiggen, in the north-east, beyond Bygdin lake, the Gjende Alps appear, behind which is the Nautgardstinden massif.

It is very worthwhile to continue on to the highest point of the **Skinneggen** (1607m). To do so, we follow the clear path southward onto the next rise (1575m), and after a short, intermediate descent, reach the highest elevation. Back at Utsikten, we follow the marked mountain path down to the west to the **Tyinholmen** Høyfjellshotell on the northern bay of the Tyin reservoir. From there, we take the bus back to the starting point.

This view looks back to the Eidsbugarden on Bygdin lake.

32 Synshorn, 1475m and Heimre Fagerdalshøi, 1510m

From Bygdin up to Synshorn

Bygdin – Synshorn – Heimre Fagerdalshø – Bygdisheim – Bygdin

Location: Vang; see walk 31.

Starting point: Bygdin Høyfjellshotell (1065m) on Lake Bygdin, on the stretch of Riksvei 51, Fagernes – Vågå, closed to public traffic in the winter.

Boat: The »MS Bitihorn« runs approx. from the end of June until approx. the beginning of September twice daily to Bygdin Høyfjellshotell, Torfinnsbu and Eidsbugarden.

Walking times: Bygdin – Synshorn a good 1½ hrs. (a good 3km, a good 400m. alt.), Synshorn – Heimre Fagerdalshøi – Bygdin 3 hrs., total time 4½ hrs. (13km).

Ascent: 600m.

Grade: Sure-footedness and, due to missing markers, a good sense of direction.

Hut: Bygdin Høyfjellshotell (mountain hotel with DNT discounts).

Maps: TurK 100, p. Jotunheimen; TK 50, p. 1617 IV Gjende.

This unmarked, yet relatively easy walk leads from Bygdin lake in south-east Jotunheimen up to the Synshorn (Panorama Horn) and the Heimre Fagerdalshøi, which both offer an excellent panorama of Jotunheimen, Valdresflya and Gausdal Vestfjell.

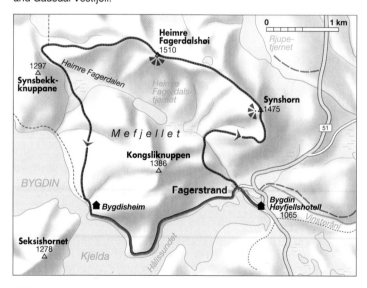

Bygdin at the foot of the Synshorn.

From the **Bygdin** Høyfjellshotell, we follow the shore road, closed to public traffic and marked with the *red T*, in the direction of Torfinnsbu (signs are posted; this private hostel is situated further west, on the northern shore of Lake Bygdin, and is also accessible by boat), and, at the end of the road, continue on an unmarked, distinct mountain path roughly straight ahead, and walk steeply uphill along the stream, which flows out from the **Heimre Fagerdalen**.

Soon, the terrain flattens out, and we cross the stream and reach **Synshorn** (1475m); to the east, the Valdresflya spreads out with the Vinstri chain of lakes.

From Synshorn, we head on to the north-west, without a trail, into a hollow with a lake, before beginning the ascent to the **Heimre Fagerdalshøi** (1510m). Here, especially the view of the sea of peaks of the Gjende Alps. From the summit, we travel downward in a roughly north-west direction to the nameless peak P 1474, where we soon find a stream and follow it down to the left (west), until we find a *T*-marked mountain path leading down from the Valdresflya Ungdomsherberge.

The path guides us, with a few splendid views of Bygdin lake, to the **Bygdis-heim** guesthouse. From there, we follow the *T* markers along the shore on the road closed to public traffic back to **Bygdin** Høyfjellshotell.

33 Skaget, 1686m

On the »Kilimanjaro« of Gausdal Vestfjell

Storeskag – Skaget – Storeskag

Location: The community of Øystre Slidre in the eastern Norwegian Fylke Oppland stretches from the Valdresflya to the Synnefjell, from Begnatal to Gausdal Vestfjell.

Starting point: DNT hut Storeskag (1127m); from Riksvei 51 Fagernes – Valdresflya – Vågå, turn off at the Heggenes Stavkirke in the direction of Skaget, and subsequently turn off once again in the direction of Skaget.

Walking times: Storeskag – Skaget a good 2 hrs., Skaget – Storeskag 2 hrs., total time 4 hrs (11km).

Ascent: 600m.

Grade: Sure-footedness, good sense of orientation, in a few spots, basic climbing knowledge is necessary.

Hut: DNT hut Storeskag (15 berths, no provisions); the hut has street access and is often »occupied«.

Maps: TurK 100, p. Jotunheimen; TK 50, p. 1617 I Sikkilsdalen and 1717 IV Espedalen.

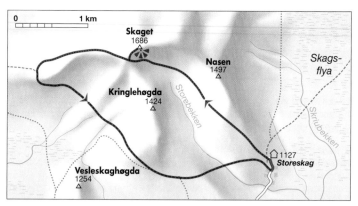

The Skaget is the highest and most distinct elevation (skage = jut out) of the plateau-like mountain countryside of Gausdal Vestfjell in the south-eastern outskirts of Jotunheimen. The summit plateau offers an accordingly enormous panorama which spans from Jotunheimen to Dovrefjell, Rondane and to Gaustatoppen. On the ascent to the summit, expect a short area where climbing is necessary, otherwise the walk is easy.

The starting point is the **Storeskag** hut (1127m) on the south-eastern foot of the Skaget. From here, the ascent route on the treeless mountain is already visible. The mountain path leads up along the slope of the eastern Skaget foothill of **Nasen** and reaches the end portion of the steep valley, from which the Storebekken stream flows. Above, we walk underneath the summit

View from Skaget of the plateau-like stretch of Gausdal Vestfjell and beyond to Jotunheimen.

plateau cliffs to the left (westward) and cross the crest between Skaget and Kringlehøgda, until a fantastic panorama opens up beyond the plateau to Jotunheimen, spotted with small mountain tops.

Once this panorama comes into view, we find ourselves roughly on the west-southwest edge of the summit plateau, and must now search for a path to the top. There are no markers here, but the steep ascent path is hard to miss. After climbing through a rocky area, we walk over the fairly expansive peak area of the **Skaget** (1686m), which offers a fabulous view: To the north-east, the view spans over Espedalen and Gudbrandsdalen over to the Rondane; in the south-west, the Synnfjell is very close to the border of Gausdal Vestfjell (and to the left of it, the Ormtjørnskampen); far off to the south, the dome of Gausta can be seen in good visibility, and in the north-west, the highest peaks of the north stretch their spiked heads up from glaciers. The name Jotunheimen, Realm of the Giants, is easy to understand for this area when viewing this vista from Skaget.

We leave the summit using the same rocky »climbing« stretch which guided us up, and keep a bit to the east at first, until we reach an obvious path at peak P 1584 which leads down to the south-east. This path merges into the *red-T* marked main hiking route a short time later. We follow it down to the starting point.

34 Veslesmeden, 2015m

From Rondvassbu to the Veslesmeden

Spranget – Rondvassbu – Veslesmeden – Nordvika / Rondvatnet – Rondvassbu – Spranget

Location: Otta, in the community of Sel, lies in the Fylke Oppland, and is the centre of the northern Gudbrandsdalen; railway station. In the south-west of the town, in the corner of the mouth of the Otta and Lågen, the Tokampen rises up, on whose peak is a defence structure stemming from the times of the migration of peoples, and which offers an excellent view of the Rondane. The panoramic neighbouring peak, Pillarguri, is named after a woman who in 1612 blew into a lur, signalling the Gudbrandsdøler farmers to destroy a Scottish mercenary army that had been marching toward them; Pillarguri is the coat-of-arms figure of Sel.

Starting point: Spranget car park (1080m), east-north-east of Otta at the end of the toll road which begins at Mysuseter.

Walking times: Spranget car park – Rondvassbu about 1 hr. (5km, 200m. alt.), Rondvassbu – Veslesmeden 3 hrs. (7km, 850m. alt.), Veslesmeden – Nordvika 2 hrs. (6km), Rondvassbu – Spranget approx. 1 hr. (5km, 50m. alt.), total time a good 7 hrs. (23km).

Ascent: 1100m.

Grade: Sure-footedness, good physical condition.

Hut: Rondvassbu (1173m), car-free DNT mountain hotel in the national park (128 beds; self-serviced hut without provisions as an extension; small tent camping area).

Map: TurK 100, p. Rondane; TK 50, p. 1718 I Rondane.

This primarily very panoramic walk leads through impressive mountain terrain into the heart of the Rondane National Park and onto the vista-rich summit of Veslesmeden; the descent leads to the northern bay of Rondvatnet lake, where the water taxi brings us back to the mountain hotel in the late afternoon (departure times are posted in Rondvassbu).

The starting point is the hikers' car park on **Spranget** (1080m), which is very large for Norwegian standards, in the direct vicinity of the border to the national park on a wide, uninhabited plateau with a fantastic view: 17 Rondane main peaks stand in a wide curve. The eye-catchers in the north-east are the highest Rondane peaks of Storronden (2178m) and, behind it to the left, Rondslottet (2178m), while the view to the south-west spans to Jotunheimen, where we can make out the Glittertind and Kvitingskjølen as the most apparent elevations.

The Spranget is a small, rocky gorge (accessible in a few minutes via the path which turns off to the north from the car park), which bears this name because the Store Ula river used to have to be jumped over here. However, erosion has caused one of the cliff walls to collapse, and a large, broken-off boulder now lies in the middle of the river. If you follow the river from Spranget about 20 minutes down-river, you will reach the **Bruresløret** waterfall, in whose vicinity historic reindeer trap pits can be found.

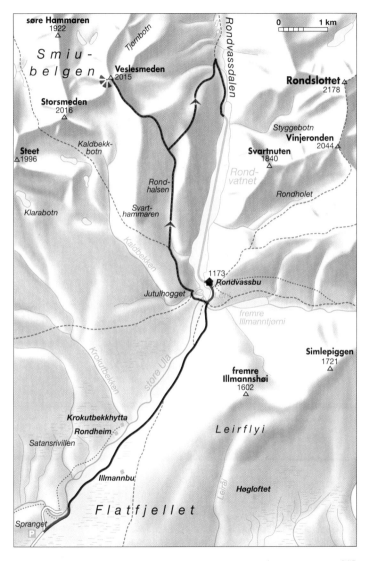

søre Hammaren
1922

S m i u -

b e l g e n

Tjørnbotn

Rondvassdalen

0   1 km

Veslesmeden
2015

Rondslottet
2178

Storsmeden
2016

Styggebotn

Vinjeronden
2044

Kaldbekk-
botn

Svartnuten
1840

Rond-
vatnet

Steet
1996

Rond-
halsen

Rondholet

Klarabotn

Svart-
hammaren

Kaldbekken

1173

Jutulhogget

Rondvassbu

fremre
Illmanntjørni

Simlepiggen
1721

Krokutbekken

store Ula

fremre
Illmannshøi
1602

Krokutbekkhytta

Rondheim

L e i r f l y i

Satansrivillen

Leirå

Illmannbu

Høgloftet

F l a t f j e l l e t

Spranget
P

The Rondvassbu hostel on Rondvatnet is not accessible by car, but can be easily reached by bicycle on the transport road.

The bicycle-accessible transport road between the **Spranget car park** and the mountain hotel Rondvassbu is the top recommendation for reaching the centre of Rondane National Park. The picturesque area north-west of the river, with its Smiubelgin massif (to which our destination, Veslesmeden, belongs) only seems like an alternate route at first glance: Due to the Satansrivillen, among other bogs not entered on the maps, it is very wet there, and further up, the terrain becomes very full of scree. The transport road is accordingly very well-visited, especially on sunny weekends during the main season.

We follow the transport road along the Store Ula river until shortly before reaching the mountain hotel **Rondvassbu** (or we take a short side-trip to Rondvassbu, in order to find out the return departure times of the water taxi), and then turn off down towards the Store Ula river; in doing so, we reach the remains of a foundation of the former Rørosvegen overnight hut. We cross the river on the foot-bridge and walk along the *T*-marked path up to the right (in the direction of »Dørålseter«) to the impressive **Jutulhogget** canyon, whose outlet is also crossed over a foot-bridge. Due to the danger of falling rock, we do not recommend entering the legendary canyon, which is said to have been carved out by a giant (jutul). At the turnoff in the path, which we reach soon after passing Jutulhogget, we turn diagonally to the right in the direction of »Veslesmeden« head upwards in the scree-filled, mountain valley-like, waterless hollow, **Rondhalsen**. This boulder-strewn mountain valley, in which one can actually see nothing but boulders covered with lichen, can be considered tough, but the marked trail then forks once again, and the final sprint begins: We turn left and pass an old, stone hunting stand, then, on a stretch which at times is very steep but very panoramic, reach the **Veslesmeden** (2015m), which is surrounded by four cirques covered in residual glaciers, and which is one of the most panoramic of the Rondane mountains. The most prominent eye-catchers on the other side of the Rondvatnet cleft include the Rondslottet massif, the peak trio of Digerronden, Midtronden and Høgronden, as well as – on the other side of the Dørålseter in the north – the Stygghøin range and, directly in the south-west, the Storsmede, the highest Smiubelgen peak.

From the summit, we turn back to the fork in the Rondhalsen mountain valley, turn left here, and soon descend on a panoramic trail into the Rondvassdalen. There, we find the *T*-marked route from Dørålseter – Rondvatnet and follow it down to the right to the ships' landing on the northern bay (Nordvika) of the lake, and take the water taxi back to **Rondvassbu**. The return route to the **car park** follows the same way in.

On the way to the Rondvassbu hostel, we see the Veslesmeden rising in the background to the right.

35 Rondslottet, 2178m

Over the highest Rondane peak to Bjørnhollia

Rondvassbu – Rondslottet – Bjørnhollia – Rondvassbu

Location: Otta, see walk 34.
Starting point: Mountain hotel Rondvassbu, 1173m, on Rondvatnet. It is a good 1 hr. from the Spranget car park to here (see walk 34).
Walking times: Rondvassbu – Rondslottet 4–5 hrs., Rondslottet – Bjørnhollia 4–5 hrs., Bjørnhollia – Rondvassbu 4–5 hrs., total time 13–15 hrs. (47km). For the return route to the Spranget car park a good 1 hr. additionally.
Ascent: 1300m.
Grade: Knowledge of the weather, sure-foo-

tedness in steep scree and boulder terrain (partly exposed), good physical condition.
Huts: Rondvassbu (1173m), DNT mountain hotel in the national park (128 beds; self-serviced hut without provisions as an extension; small tent camping area); Bjørnhollia (914m), car-free DNT mountain hotel (90 beds; self-serviced hut without provisions as an extension).
Maps: TurK 100, p. Rondane; TK 50, p. 1718 I Rondane and 1818 IV Atnsjøen.

You should plan on at least one overnight stay for this magnificent hut and summit walk in Rondane National Park.

From the **Spranget car park**, we walk, as in walk 34, to the **Rondvassbu** hotel on **Rondvatnet** (1167m) in the heart of the national park. Rondvassbu is recommended for overnight accommodation, before crossing the Rondlottet the next day. Officially, this walk is slated at 9 hours, but the descent must

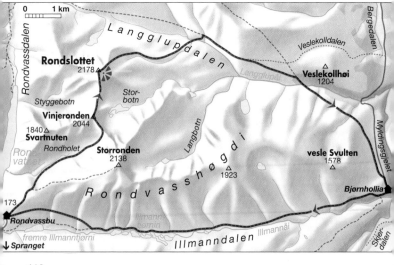

The final ascent to the Rondslottet summit is rich in scree and panorama.

be done in a timely manner. We do not recommend crossing the Rondslottet in poor visibility and/or precipitation. If even just a small amount of snow has fallen during the night, the walk becomes dangerous. If there is precipitation or if it has snowed, do not cross the Rondslottet, but rather, head northwards along the *T*-marked route over the western shore of the lake and then into the Langglupdalen. A further alternative route to shorten the walk is via the water taxi; it runs between Rondvassbu and the northern bay of the Rondvatnet, where you follow the *T* markers and directional signs straight ahead to »Bjørnhollia« and then turn right into Langglupdalen valley.

Beyond Rondvassbu, the *T* markers lead up a steep slope. Above, at the fork in the path, we turn diagonally to the left, pass the Storronden turnoff, and then keep in an upward direction in the cirque valley **Rondholet**. After a scree-covered, steep ascent, the panoramic ribbon between Rondholet and the impressive cirque Storbotn provide a good place to rest, before undertaking the boulder-strewn ascent to the panoramic summit of the **Vinjeronden**. After an interim descent through the boulder and slate slab-covered northern flank of the Vinjeronden, the steep, extremely panoramic final ascent to the **Rondslottet** (2178m) begins. In the north, we can make out the Snøhetta (Dovrefjell) on the horizon.

From the summit, there is a long descent into **Langglupdalen**, by walking down to **Bjørnhollia**. Bjørnhollia is a pretty hut in a diverse environment, ideal for a day of rest.

The last leg of the walk leads through **Illmanndalen** = Villmanndalen to **Rondvatnet** and back to the **starting point**. The reindeer trap pits can be seen approximately in the middle of this valley.

36 On Storronden, 2138m

On the second-highest Rondane summit

Rondvassbu – Storronden – Rondvassbu

Location: Otta, see walk 34.
Starting point and hut: DNT mountain hotel Rondvassbu (1173m), see walk 35.
Walking times: Rondvassbu – Storronden almost 3 hrs., return route 2 hrs., total time almost 5 hrs. (8km).

Ascent: 1000m.
Grade: Sure-footedness in rocky terrain and on scree (almost the whole way), good physical condition, knowledge of weather.
Map: TurK 100, p. Rondane; TK 50, p. 1718 I Rondane.

From the DNT mountain hotel Rondvassbu, this panoramic walk leads onto Storronden, the second-highest of the Rondane peaks. Although almost 1000 metres of altitude of almost continuous rocky slab and scree terrain must be surmounted, Storronden is the most frequented summit in Rondane National Park.

In back of the DNT mountain hotel **Rondvassbu** (1173m), the *red-T* marked trail winds steeply in serpentine curves up the slope, and reaches a turnoff shortly after the terrain flattens out: in the east, the Illmanndalen comes into view, through which the path to the staffed hut Bjørnhollia leads (see walk 35). This valley is bordered at the outset by the southern flank of the Storronden.

Our Storronden trail branches off to the left at this point and leads on a constant downhill slope to the beginning of the western ridge of Storronden. There, we reach another turnoff, marked with signs, which leads in the

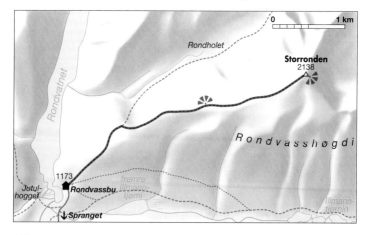

During the ascent of Storronden, we see the highest mountains of northern Europe to the west.

direction of Rondslottet, while we remain on the western ridge of the Storronden. The marked, scree-strewn trail leads on a continuous uphill grade; along the way, a stone hunting stand offers a resting place. What at first looks like the summit is in fact not: There is still a last stretch uphill, before we reach the summit of **Storronden** (2138m). The ascent in the virtually endless scree can seem tough; however, the panorama, also visible during the climb, is one of the finest.

On the summit, the view encompasses the Langbotn cirque, to which the summit area drops vertically; in the north, the Storbotn cirque separates the Storronden from the Rondslottet massif, the Rondslottet rising to the right beyond the Langglupdalen as the third-highest Rondane peak of the Høgronden. Further back in the north-east, we see the crescent-shaped summit ridge of the Sølnkletten in Alvdal Vestfjell, and in the south-west, the Norefjell, 185km away, can be seen in good visibility. The snow-covered, 2000-metre mountains of the Jotunheimen rise to the west. One of the most remarkable eye-catchers in the immediate vicinity is **Jutulhogget** canyon (Giant Notch, see walk 34) where the Kaldbekken flows into the Rondvatnet. The stream drops in a waterfall between the sheer, wall-like cliffs, and, at its outlet out of the canyon, has deposited a delta-like alluvial cone through which a number of stream branches run. This natural structure can best be viewed from the elevations in the lower area of Storronden.

The return route follows the same route used to get there.

37 Høgronden, 2114m

To the dead-ice holes and Høgronden

Dørålseter – Skranglehaugan – Høgronden – Dørålseter

Starting from the Dørålseter hostel, situated in a kind of glacial garden countryside, this walk leads to the Skranglehaugan dead-ice holes and then over a panoramic mountain plateau, accentuated by the green and white colour of various lichen, before the ascent to Høgronden, the third-highest

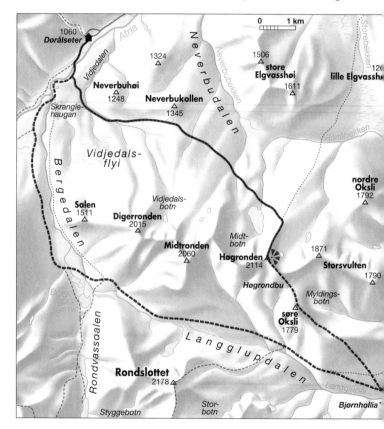

Location: The community of Dovre is situated in the Fylke Oppland and encompasses the northern portion of Rondane National Park, the northern Gudbrandsdalen and the highest part of the Dovrefjell National Park, with its Snøhetta (2286m). The largest towns are Dombås and Dovre.

Starting point: Dørålseter hostel (1060m) at the end of the »Dørålsetervegen« toll road, which branches off of Riksvei 27 between Folldal and Atnbrua.

Walking times: Dørålseter – Skranglehaugan almost ½ hr., Skrangehaugan – Høgronden a good 4 hrs., return route 3½ hrs., total time 8 hrs. (20km).

Ascent: 1250m.

Grade: Sure-footedness in partially very rocky and boulder-strewn terrain, which is exposed and requires the use of hands.

Hut: Privately-staffed Dørålseter hostel (1060m), DNT discount).

Maps: TurK 100, p. Rondane; TK 50, p. 1718 I Rondane.

Alternative route: If you do not need to get back to the starting point on the same day, you can follow the signs from the summit marker steeply down to the DNT hostel Bjørnhollia, and after an overnight stay, walk the valley route between Høgronden and Rondslottet back to Dørålseter; Høgronden – Bjørnhollia 4 hrs., Bjørnhollia – Dørålseter 7 hrs.

Rondane summit, begins. The ascent is steep and leads through boulder-strewn terrain in which you have to use your hands from time to time.

From the **Dørålseter** hostel, we follow the *red-T* marked route along the slope of **Dørålen** valley upwards, go down to the Atna river at the first turnoff, cross it on a short suspension bridge, and come to another turnoff. Here, we follow the sign to »Høgronden« steeply up the moraine flank, and reach the **Skranglehaugan**: To the right, a bizarre dead-ice funnel landscape opens up, with up to 50-metre deep, funnel-like hollows, some filled with water.

The Skranglehaugan, as the Atna valley, was created at the end of the last Ice Age. Where the Atna flows today, a glacier, accompanied by moraines, pushed its way through the valley 10,000 years ago; when the climate became warmer, the ice covering the northern Rondane slope flowed down in the direction of the valley ice river.

The mighty valley ice river blocked the path of the ice flows coming down from the mountains, the last of which depositing sand and scree in front of the valley ice river, thus building the high flank over which we climbed from the Atna Valley to the Skranglehaugen. At the same time, the ice flowing down from the mountains shattered in the collision with the valley ice flow; giant blocks of ice broke off and were enclosed by scree as »dead ice«, unable to continue flowing; when these dead ice blocks subsequently melted, the funnels (hollows) were created.

The *T*-marked path leads past the hollows and over the panoramic mountain plateau **Vidjedalsflyi**, before passing the impressive **Midtbotn** cirque and beginning the stony ascent onto **Høgronden** (2114m). Whereas up to this point, the »only« vista was to the east in the direction of Alvdal Vestfjell, now the summit offers a magnificent view of the Langglupdalen and beyond to Rondslottet.

38 Store Sølnkletten, 1827m

Crest walk over the highest mountain of the Alvdal Vestfjell

Follandsvangen – Store Sølnkletten – Breisjøseter – Follandsvangen

Location: The community of Alvdal is located in the eastern Norwegian Fylke Hedmark on both sides of the Glåma River.
Starting point: Follandsvangen hostel (890m) in Sølndalen west of Alval; accessible via a toll road which branches off of Riksvei 3 Hamar – Elverum – Kopang – Alvdal in Alvdal.
Walking times: Follandsvangen – Store Sølnkletten 5 hrs., Store Sølnkletten – Breisjøseter 2 hrs., Breisjøseter – Follandsvangen 3 hrs., total time 10 hrs (23km).
Ascent: 1200m.
Grade: Knowledge of the weather, good sense of orientation and lack of vertigo in terrain which is partly very steep and strewn with rocks and boulders.
Hut: Breisjøseter hostel (48 beds).
Maps: TurK 100, p. Rondane or – better – TurK 75, p. Sölnkletten; TK 50, p. 1619 III Alvdal and 1818 IV Atnsjøen.
Alternative route: If you want to avoid the steep, scree-strewn crest walk, which can seem exposed in places, go directly to the Breisjøseter hostel; the ascent from there to Store Sølnkletten is not as badly exposed.

This walk leads from Sølndalen over the crest of the double-peaked Store Sølnkletten, the highest elevation of Alvdal Vestfjell, to the Breisjøseter hostel, in which you can stay overnight. The hostel has no road access, but is a popular destination of mountain bikers, who use the transport road, closed off to public traffic, starting at Atnsjøen Lake.

Below the **Follandsvangen**, we cross the Sølna River on a bridge, pass a turnoff in the path (the path leads downstream to the Franksætra hostel), and walk straight on through birch trees past **Vesle Follandstjørna** lake in the direction of Sølnkletten / Breisjøseter.

The impressive double-peaked silhouette of Sølnkletten, seen from Muen.

A short distance later, after passing under a power line, we reach another turnoff in the trail: to the left (east), the path branches off to the DNT self-serviced hut Korsberghytta, whereas we continue along straight on, following the *T* markers in the direction of Breisjøseter, and gradually leave the birch wood at the foot of the Vesle Sølnklettern. In the birch zone up to this point, the terrain can be intermittently damp and boggy.

After crossing the Sølnsjøbekken stream, we begin the panoramic ascent, first at a moderate incline, up to a further turnoff in the path (straight on, the way leads along the foot of the Store Sølnkletten directly to Breisjøseter), which branches off in a steep ascent to the Store Sølnkletten. It follows the crest line with a singular view up to the western peak (1690m). From there, the path leads steeply and strewn with boulders downhill in the col between the twin peaks, before we begin the final ascent, also very steep, to the main peak of the **Store Sølnkletten** (1827m).

The most remarkable eye-catcher in the north-east, beyond the Glåma Valley, is the Tron, to the right of it, we can make out Elgpiggen in Fremundsmarka in the background, and further to the south-east, the long Rendalssølen, while in the south, the Muen rises; the Rondane 2000-metre peaks in the west cover much of Jotunheimen, but in good visibility, you should be able to see the Gjende Alps and Surtningssui; the eye-catcher to the north-west, on the other hand, is Snøhetta in Dovrefjell.

From the summit, a steep descent of 600 metres in altitude begins, until we reach the path crossing over from Korsberghytta (east). We follow it to the right (west), down to the **Breisjøseter** hostel on **Breisjøen** lake. From there, we follow the *T* markers on the path at the foot of Store Sølnkletten back to **Follandsvangen**.

39 Muen, 1424m

Panoramic scree pyramid in Ringebulfjellet

Muvatnet – Muen – Muvatnet

Location: Ringebu, railway station in the Gudbrandsdalen, is the suburb of the community of the same name in the eastern Norwegian Fylke Oppland. The stave church (approx. 1200) was rebuilt in the post-Reformation age. On the grounds of Dale Gudbrands gård (museum) in Hundorp, Saint Olav held his famous Ting, through which he led Chief Dale-Gudbrand to Christianity; Gudbrandsdalen is said to be named after Dale-Gudbrand.

Starting point: Parking bay (1060m) on

Lake Muvatnet north of Ringebu on Riksvei 27 Ringebu – Enden – Folldal.

Walking times: Muvatnet – Muen, a good 1 hr., return route 1 hr., total time 2 hrs. (4km).

Ascent: 350m.

Grade: Scree and boulders require sure-footedness.

Map: TK 50, p. 1818 III Ringebu.

Alternative route: A side-trip to the panoramically-situated DNT self-serviced hut Gråhøgdbu (8 berths) takes almost 1 hr. (3km), there and back a good 1½ hrs.

The pyramid-shaped Muen is the highest mountain of the Ringebufjellet, one of the most diverse and well-visited (huts and holiday village) mountain area between Gudbrandsdalen and the eastern Rondane foothills. The summit

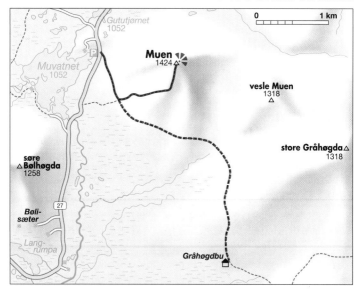

Ascent of Muen.

allows an excellent panorama of the surrounding mountains. The route is rocky in parts, partially strewn with boulders, and requires a bit of co-ordination when jumping from boulder to boulder, stone to stone, which is why 1 hour should actually be planned for the 2-km ascent. Since, despite the markers, the path was not always clearly visible among the scree, the sparse vegetation was damaged by illegally-installed steps. The meticulously exactly placed markers are intended to allow the vegetation to recover (»revegetering«).

At the starting point near **Muvatnet**, the treeless mountain (muen = haystack) and the ascent route are in view. We cross the national road and, at the »Muen 1 time« sign, follow a washed-out way for a brief distance in a south-easterly direction uphill up to the first turnoff. Straight on, the trail leads to the DNT hut Gråhøgdbu, whereas we turn off to the left onto the scree-covered flank. To compensate for the climb through the scree, a view which becomes more and more impressive along the way opens up in the direction of Jotunheimen. Then we reach the summit of **Muen** (1424m), which is one of the mountains with the most stone markers in Norway: The relatively small peak is covered in stone markers, through and through. The panorama is excellent, and the most remarkable eye-catcher in the north is the fascinating crescent silhouette of the double-peaked Store Sølnketten in Alvdal Vestfjell, and in the north-west, the 2000-metre peaks of the Rondane can be seen.

40 Ormtjørnskampen, 1128m

Through the Ormtjørnskampen primeval forest National Park

Holsbrua – Ormtjørnskampen – Holsbrua

Location: The community of Gausdal is situated in the Fylke Oppland west of Gudbrandsdalen; in addition to the Gausdal, it encompasses the south-eastern part of the plateau-like mountain region of Gausdal Vestfjell. The potholes, called Helvete, in the valley of the Dritua are considered among the largest in Norway. With the aid of exhibits and nature trails, the Kittilbu Utmark Museum on the Vestfjellvegen a few kilometres to the east of the starting point provides information on 8000 years of culture and nature in Gausdal Vestfjell.

Starting point: Parking bay (810m) on Vestfjellvegen in the spot where a private road branches off to the west at the Dokka

bridge (Holsbrua). The Vestfjellvegen is the pass road from Vestre Gausdal to Fagernes which is closed in winter.

Walking times: Holsbrua – Ormtjørnskampen a good 2 hrs., return route 2 hrs., total time 4 hrs. (11km).

Ascent: 350m.

Grade: Sure-footedness and a good sense of orientation are necessary.

Huts: None along the way.

Map: TK 50, p. 1717 II Synnfjell.

Alternative route: From the stone marker (1000m), you can continue along the foot of Dokkampen westward and then climb up Dokkampen; depending on the water situation in the bogs, 2–3 hrs. there and back.

This walk leads through Ormtjørnskampen National Park, in which one of the largest pristine spruce forest areas in Norway is located. The ascent up to the Ormtjørnskampen summit offers an excellent view, and, in good weather, a small lake at the foot of Dokkampen invites you for a swim.

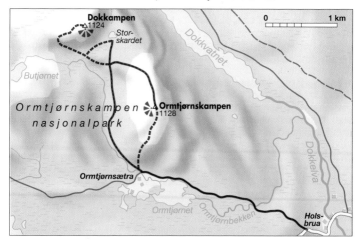

View from Dokkampen to Orntjørnskampen, on the right the primeval forest area.

From the parking bay near the **Holsbrua** bridge over the Dokka river, we follow a private toll road, closed to public traffic, for almost an hour roughly to the west; the road is easily accessible by bicycle. Shortly after the road has passed Lake **Ormtjørnet**, our trail branches off to the right before the Ormtjørnbekken stream, into the primeval forest national park. The path snakes along through the forest near fallen, strewn-about tree trunks. The giant trees, some up to 300 years old, are left to their own devices; the forest grows without the intervention of humans; wildly-proliferating vegetation, thick underwood and fallen tree trunks hinder the way forward off the path. The forest floor is covered by carpets of blueberry bushes.

When the path emerges from the evergreen forest, the Synnfjell, with its snow-covered Spåtind, is visible between fjell birches, and in the north, we can make out the steeply-dropping Dokkampen (1124m). A stone marker at almost 1000 m indicates the spot where the path branches off to the east, up to Ormtjørnskampen, and at the same time, beneath the eastern break-off of Dokkampen, a small lake is visible, which is an excellent place to rest.

The col between Ormtjørnkampen and Dokkampen, called **Storskardet**, has large patches of moorland. The panoramic path is free from moorland, and leads over the northern ridge to the summit of **Ormtjørnskampen** (1128m). The panorama includes the lakes, forests and mountains of the plateau from Gausdal Vestfjell and over to Rondane.

For the **descent**, the same route is recommended; the path on the southern slope is partially very steep and exposed.

41 Spåtind, 1414m

Panoramic walk on the Synnfjell

Lenningen – Spåtind – Lenningen

On the Synnfjell.

Location: The community of Nordre Land lies in the eastern Norwegian Fylke Oppland on both sides of Dokka valley. The suburb is Dokka, on the splendid delta where the Dokka and Etna meet in Randsfjord. Dokka is the location of the Lands Museum, with over 20 antique houses. The 4000-year old rock drawings near the Møllerstugufossen waterfall in Etna valley above Dokka depict ghost elks.

Starting point: Lenningen Hyttesenter (1040m), rental hut grounds on the Vestfjellvegen pass road between Vestre Gausdal and Fagernes; the *T*-marked path begins a few minutes of walking north of the hut grounds.

Walking times: Lenningen – Spåtind, a good 2 hrs., return route 2 hrs., total time 4 hrs. (15km).

Ascent: 400m.

Grade: Sure-footedness is necessary.

Hut: In Lenningen, you can buy food and rent relatively expensive huts.

Map: TK 50, p. 1717 II Synnfjell.

Alternative route: Spåtind is covered with a number of marked and unmarked paths. If you walk down the *T*-marked path to the south-east, you will reach the Nørdstelia hostel and can stay there overnight; however, parts of this route are extremely boggy. Almost 3 hrs. from the summit to the hut, and a good 3 hrs. for the return route.

Above the tree line, this comfortable walk, with the exception of a few boggy passages, leads to Spåtind, which offers a unique panorama. Spåtind is the highest elevation of the Synnfjellvidda, a widely boggy plateau in the south of the Gausdal Vestfjell on the border to Nordre Land.

From the rental and holiday hut grounds of **Lenningen**, we follow the *Vestfjellvegen* road a few minutes to the north, until a *red-T* marked path branches off to the right (east) in the direction of Spåtind. At the outset, the path leads through boggy terrain and fjell birch wood, but soon the panoramic portion of the walk begins: in the north, the Ormtjørnskampen in the national park of the same name comes into view; to the west of it, we see Skaget and the other mountains in Gausdal Vestfjell; beyond, the peaks of Jotunheimen rise up, and the higher the trail leads, the more encompassing the view becomes.

Shortly after passing the small Hasatjørnet lake, we reach the stone marker on the summit of **Spåtind** (1414m). When visibility is good, Gaustatoppen can be seen 150km further to the south-west, and in the south, the large Randsfjord Lake is visible; Mjøsa lake shimmers to the south-east, and in the north, the Rondane peaks border the horizon.

The descent is made along the same route.

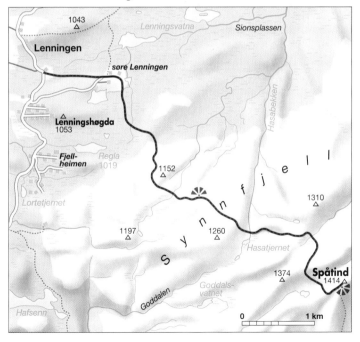

42 To Høgevarde, 1459m

Panoramic walk in Norefjell

Norefjellstua – Augunshaug – Høgevarde – Norefjellstua

Location: The winter sport town of Noresund (133m) is situated on the Krøderen
reservoir at the eastern foot of the Norefjell in
the southern Norwegian community of
Krødsherad in Fylke Buskerud. Ever since
the Winter Olympics of 1952, the Norefjell
has been one of the most popular and
modern alpine and cross-country ski areas
in Norway.

Starting point: Car park at Norefjellstua
(approx. 820m) at the end of the »Norefjell«
toll road west-northwest of Noresund; turn
off in Noresund in the direction of Norefjell.

Access via E 7 Oslo / Hønefoss – Noresund
– Geilo.

Walking times: Norefjellstua – Augunshaug
a good 1 hr., Augunshaug – Høgevarde
almost 2 hrs., return route 3 hrs., total time
6 hrs. (22km).

Ascent: 750m.

Grade: Sure-footedness, good physical
condition and knowledge of the weather.

Hut: Høgevarde Turisthytte, DOT self-serviced hut (27 berths), staffed at Easter.

Map: TurK 50, p. Norefjell og Eggedalsfjella.

This comfortable walk leads above the tree line with a magnificent view over
the mighty quartzite ridge of the Norefjell between the Krøderen reservoir
and the Eggedalen valley area. The crowning glory is the view from Høgevarde: In a gigantic panorama, 40,000km^2 of southern Norway unfolds. It is
especially recommended, especially in good visibility, to stay overnight in
the hut on the lake at the foot of the mountain.

West of **Norefjellstua** (with an opportunity to stop), the *T*-marked path
begins, which at first ascends, rocky and steep, between fjell birch wood,
before the comfortable panoramic walk begins a few minutes above the tree
line, initially impaired by ski lifts (the *T* path does not follow the chair lift, but
rather runs parallel to it on the mountainside for a stretch). After crossing a
foothill of Ramnås, the destination of the first leg of the journey approaches,
the high ridge of **Augunshaug** (1342m), upon which, for the first time, we can
see our ultimate destination, the Høgevarde Pyramids. Augunshaug (a short,
unmarked side-trip to the right, 10 minutes) offers a beautiful vista.

From Augunshaug, the *T* markers guide us along a panoramic route further
through the fjell, partially covered in grass, partially in scree. Soon after
crossing the Grindefjell, we reach the **Høgevarde Turisthytta** on Høgvardet-
jørnet lake at the foot of **Høgevarde** (1459m), upon whose summit we will
arrive via the north-west ridge fifteen minutes later. From the battlements of
Jotunheimen, the view sweeps over to the mountaintops of the Rondane,
from the Hardangerjøkulen glacier to Gaustatoppen, the only peak offering a
more extensive view than Høgevarde. A panorama orientation plaque names
the various points in view.

The **return route** follows the same route; there is no alternative.

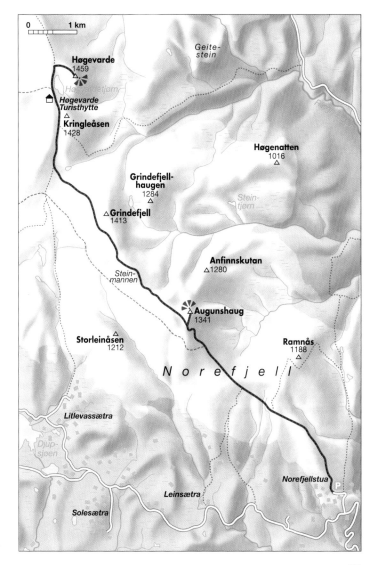

0   1 km

Høgevarde
1459

Høgevarde Turisthytte

Kringleåsen
1428

Geite-stein

Høgenatten
1016

Grindefjell-haugen
1284

Grindefjell
1413

Stein-tjørn

Anfinnskutan
1280

Stein-mannen

Augunshaug
1341

Storleinåsen
1212

N o r e f j e l l

Ramnås
1188

Litlevassætra

Djup-sjøen

Norefjellstua

P

Leinsætra

Solesætra

43 To the legendary Andersnatten, 733m

Short walk to a panoramic mountain overlooking the Eggedal

Andersnattjørnet – Andersnatten – Andersnattjørnet

Location: The community of Sigdal is situated in the southern Norwegian Fylke Buskerund and encompasses the valley areas of Eggedal and Sigdal, as well as parts of the Norefjell.
In Prestfoss, you can find the Eggedal and Sigdal Outdoor Museum. A few kilometres to the south, the church (17th cent.) of Vatnås is located at the legendary Olav's Spring. Access via RV 287 Åmot – Sigdal – Hallingdal.

Starting point: Car park at Andersnattjørnet lake (414m) on a toll road which branches off of Riksvei 287 at Nedre Eggedal.
Walking times: Andersnattjørnet – Andersnatten 1 hr., return route 1 hr., total time 2 hrs. (4km).
Ascent: 350m.
Grade: Sure-footedness in partially boggy, partially rocky and steep terrain.
Maps: TurK 50, p. Norefjell og Eggedalsfjella; TK 50, p. 1715 III Eggedal.

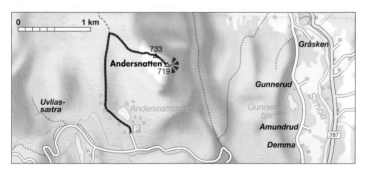

This short, beautiful walk follows a typical fjell path, parts of which lead through woods, onto Andersnatten, a legendary granite giant high above the Eggedal, through which the Simoa flows. The rocky walls of the Andersnatten are well-known to climbers (and ice climbers). Its summit area allows an impressive view, and in Norwegian painting, it has been a common motif ever since Theodor Kittelsen. During the drive along the national road, the two legendary »white lines« are visible on the east flank of the mountain: A giant named Anders is said to have once travelled through the eastern wall on skis with a child on his back – the white veins in the rock are the tracks of this fantastic ride.

The starting point is the marshy lake **Andersnattjørnet** in the forefront of the Andersnatten south-west wall. As in other southern Norwegian fjell regions

View from Andersnatten of the Sigdal valley.

not under protection, there is a holiday hut settlement here. We follow the slatted path, which is situated on the south-western shore of the lake, above the marsh, through sparse wood. Soon, the path swerves to the right (north), leaves the boggy hollow, and snakes towards the mountain, partially steep and repeatedly offering pretty vistas. The more the path gains in altitude, the more sparse the wood becomes, ultimately replaced by gnarled, isolated pine trees, digging their roots in cracks and crevices, each tree a distinctive personality.

Finally, the mountain path reaches the north-west ridge, swings to the right, and leads in a gentle ascent upwards over the rocks. Below, the marsh from where we started reflects the sky, on the other side of the woody valley hollow, the Borofjell rises up. Even on the summit plateau of the **Andersnatten** (733m), old, weathered pines stand as if frozen, ducking leeward for cover from the storm or snuggling up flat to the rock. The edge over the eastern wall is a panoramic resting place.

After the rest, we continue along the same route over rock and blueberry carpets, and through the light-flooded wood back to the **starting point**.

If you follow the toll road from here a bit further southward, you will come upon several small lakes at the foot of the Borofjell: a glorious landscape which practically screams for you to pitch your tent.

44 Bletoppen, 1342m

Mountain walk in Blefjell

Nordstul – Bletoppen – Sigridsbu – Nordstul

Location: The town of Flesberg lies in the southern Norwegian Fylke Buskerud in the valley of the River Numedalslågen on the eastern foot of the Blefjell. The stave church built around 1200 received its current appearance in 1735. Access via Riksvei 40, Kongsberg – Flesberg – Geilo.

Starting point: Car park (approx. 720m) in Blefjell at the end of the »Norstulveien« toll road south-east of Flesberg; travel from Flesberg in the direction of Kongsberg, and turn right onto Riksvei 37 in the direction Rjukan. Turn right shortly after Bølkesjø in the direction of Store Blefjell.

Walking times: Nordstul – Bletoppen about 3 hrs., return route 2 hrs., total time 5 hrs. (15km).

Ascent: 650m.

Grade: Sure-footedness in partially steep and scree and boulder-strewn terrain. On the mountain path next to the last lake, a lack of vertigo is necessary.

Hut: Sigridsbu (1000m), non-staffed KOT hut (18 berths, no provisions).

Map: TK 50, p. 1614 I Tinnsjå and 1714 IV Flesberg.

This walk leads through diverse mountain terrain with woods, lakes, streams and rocky high fjell up to the panoramic Bletoppen, the highest peak in the Blefjell on the watershed between Numedal and Tinnsjå.

The *red-T* marked path begins to the left (west) of the Storeblekiosken (kiosk) at the starting point, which we follow gently uphill and which, after crossing a hilltop, guides us to the idyllic **Sønstevatnet**, whose outflow is crossed on a fairly stable bridge. The *T* markers lead on to a second, small lake surrounded by carpets of moorland, and then enters the wood.

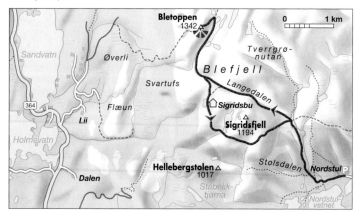

The route through the flank of the Bletoppen leads along a mountain path which at times is narrow.

After a while of silent walking, the marker branches off the path suddenly to the right, at a grotesquely deformed spruce, and a short time later, a mountain stream must be jumped over. Then, we leave the wood in the upper area of the **Nordstul** clearance and follow the *red T* marker further uphill. The path, which approximately follows the deeply-cut mountain stream, may seem steep, but the higher we get, the more beautiful the view of the chain of lakes that was our starting place becomes.

Above a small waterfall, the terrain flattens out somewhat, at the Sigridbsu turnoff, we go a few steps straight on, then turn left and head up to Langedalen, flanked by cliffs. Once we have reached the watershed (a tiny lake has formed there) – always following the *red T* – the panoramic portion of the walk begins, with an excellent view over the Tinnsjå hollows and beyond to Gausta; to the right, we see our destination, the Bletoppen, with its quartzite walls.

From the watershed, the *T* markers lead to the right, up into Bledalen, in which we pass two additional lakes. Shortly behind the last lake, the ascent begins on the left, to the expansive double-peaked plateau of **Bletoppen** (1342m), which offers a fantastic panorama.

We follow the same path back to Langedalen, and there, turn right at the first turnoff, and head up to **Sigridsbu**; there, too, there are small lakes. From the hut, the markers lead past other lakes, and at Omnsveggen passes one of the southernmost animal trap pits in Norway, then rejoins the familiar trail: Here, to the right, we can get back to the lakes and our **starting point**.

45 Styggmann, 877m

Forest and mountain walk in the Skrimfjell

Car park – Omholtsetra – Store Kongstjønet – Styggmann – car park

Location: The town of Kongsberg is situated in the Fylke Buskerund on the lower reaches of the Numedalslågen river.

Starting point: Car park (approx. 620m) at the holiday hut settlement in Omholtfjellet south of Kongsberg. Access via E 134 Oslo – Kongsberg, turn off onto Riksvei 40 Kongsberg – Larvik; from Riksvei 40, turn off after approx. 11km in the direction of Omholtfjel / Skrim, and lastly, drive along the »Skrimvelen« toll road until the car park at the end.

Walking times: Omholtsetra – Fantefjell

1 hr., Fantefjell – Styggmann almost 2 hrs., return route 3 hrs., total time 6 hrs. (20km).

Ascent: 300m.

Grade: Sure-footedness and a good sense of orientation; a few boggy passages. In woody terrain, you must pay close attention to markers and signs at turnoffs, and regularly compare the route with your map.

Huts: Kaffeebua at the starting point; the huts Darrebu (8 berths), Sørmyrsætra (9), Styggmannshytta (2) and Ivarsbu (16) are self-serviced huts without provisions.

Map: TurK 50, p. Skien – Kongsberg.

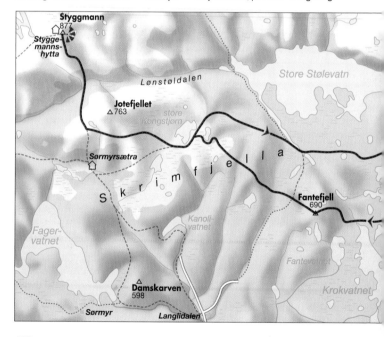

This forest and fjell walk, comfortable with the exception of a few boggy stretches, mainly guides us with excellent panoramas past several lakes, and leads through the Skrimfjell, famous for its wealth of plant and animal life (elk, lynx, beaver) as well as its diverse geology (granite, limestone, marble).

From the **car park** at the end of the toll road, we walk past Kaffebua and above it, turn off to the left onto the *blue-red* marked slab trail in the direction of »Omholtsetra«.

The path leads upward between heath vegetation and pine and fjell birch wood. To the left and right in the wood there are holiday huts. Boggy patches are covered with planks. After crossing a boggy hollow, the *blue-red* trail leads diagonally to the left on in the direction of »Styggemann«. There are now no more holiday huts, we pass the signposted **Darrebu hut** on the left, and head uphill in a blueberry-rich, sparse mountain spruce wood.

There is a point where the *blue-red* marker is so hidden that you will probably miss the turnoff to **Minnestein** and continue straight on along the *blue*-marked trail: Both Alternative routes converge again on a very panoramic hilltop. The *blue* trail, which in stretches is also the *red* trail, leads along a succession

of bogs, lakes and woods via **Fantefjell** and **Store Kongstjørnet** to the panoramic **Styggmann** (877m). This panoramic peak, with its smoothly sanded rock, is named after an »ugly / creepy man« (styggmann), who is said to have been living here for ages, but is only visible at night, which is why no physical description of him exists, and why there is even question as to whether the Styggmann is a two or four-legged creature. On the summit, we find a stone emergency hut. The view spans to Oslofjord.

The return route is identical to the way there up to the **Store Kongstjørnet** lake; from there, we continue straight on (in the direction of Ivarsbu), and at Lake **Svarttjørnet**, we go to the right, back to the starting point.

46 Himingen, 1066m

Isolated short walk onto a steep, panoramic mountain in Lifjell

Gavlesjå – Himingen – Gavlesjå

Location: The town of Notodden (population 12,500) is situated between Lifjell and Skrim in Heddalsvatnet in Telemark. Access via E 134 Drammen – Notodden – Haugesund. The largest preserved stave church (13th century) is located in Heddal, a few kilometres north-west of Notodden.

Starting point: Car park (660m) in Lifjell at the end of the »Gavlesjåvegen« toll road (where it looks like the road forks). Access from Notodden on the E 134 in the direction of Haugesund; turn off in Melås Bru in the direction of Gavlesjå Skisenter.

Walking times: Car park – Himingen a good hour, return route 1 hr., total time 2 hrs. (5km).

Ascent: 400m.

The view up to Himingen from Heddal.

Grade: Sure-footedness and lack of vertigo on a narrow path in steep terrain.

Huts: generally, none; there is a kiosk which is open seasonally at the starting point.

Map: TurK 50, p. Lifjell.

Alternative route: The view from Himingen entices the hiker to further explore the Lifjell. After descending along the same route, continue up on the continuation of the Gavlesjåvegen to the next lake, and in its northern shore area, further on to the Gavlesjå. In the southern bay area of this large lake, the path swerves to the left (eastward), keeps to the valley for a short time, then swerves to the left again, and after crossing the panoramic Rognlifjellet, reaches the familiar trail again; 3–4 hrs. for the circular walk.

This short, in spots steep and slightly exposed walk leads to the panoramic Himingen in Lifjell. This legendary mountain, which is said to be inhabited by several ghosts, offers a magnificent panorama: Gausta, Blefjell, Norefjell, Skrim and several other mountains and mountain chains of southern Norway are in view.

From the **car park** at the end of the *Gavlesjåvegen* toll road, we walk a few steps to the north in the direction of the huts, and then turn left onto the *blue*-marked path in the direction of »Himingen«.

With a view to the rocky walls of the Himingen and the few huts nestled at its foot, the path, containing wet and rocky spots, leads between fjell birch, pine, heather, and blueberries, and soon swerves away from the power line and heads for the mountain.

The ascent is steep and can seem exposed in spots. In return, the view of the chain of lakes at the starting point becomes more and more wonderful, and when the mountain path scales the eastern break-away of the summit area via a gully, an extraordinary vista of the Skrimfjella opens up.

It makes a beautiful place to rest before following the *blue* markers through another gully up to the Himingen eastern summit, where we can now also see Gaustatoppen and, far below, the Hedda, as well as the Heksfjellet diagonally to the left. Shortly thereafter, we reach the Himingen main summit (1066m). There, a surprise in the summit register awaits: Although Himingen rises above the well-visited Heddal, only about one ascent per day is recorded.

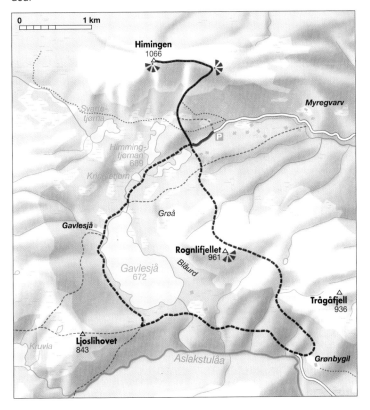

47 Gausta, 1881m

On the most panoramic mountain in Norway

Stavsrobua – Gaustahytta – Gaustatoppen – Stavsrobua

Location: The water-power station and industrial town of Rjukan is located in the Telemark community of Tinn, in the deeply-cut Vestfjorddalen between Hardangervidda and Gausta. Access via Riksvei 37 Kongsberg – Rjukan – Åmot. The vista point of Gvepseborg, with an excellent view over the valley and beyond to Gausta, is accessible via cableway.

Starting point: Car park (1180m) Stavsrobua; turn off in Dale, east of Rjukan in the direction of Tuddal / Gaustaområdet.

Walking times: Stavsrobua – Gaustatoppen a good 2½ hrs., return route 1½ hrs., total time a good 4 hrs. (10km).

Ascent: 750m. alt.

Grade: Good physical condition and sure-footedness in steep, rocky terrain; the last portion requires a lack of vertigo.

Hut: Gaustahytta, staffed SST hut (11 berths).

Map: TurK 100, p. Hardangervidda Øst; TK 50, p. IV Rjukan.

Alternative route: An ascent beginning in Svineroi to Gaustatoppen, which is steep, but with a good 2½ hrs. of climbing time, not any more time consuming. It also allows a panoramic walk around the massif.

The descent leads, with very steep passages, to the Selstalli mountain pasture in 2½ hrs; from there, you need 1½ hrs. more to walk along the northern slope of Gausta back to the starting point; total time almost 7 hrs.

The majestic Gausta rises up steeply over 1000m above the surrounding valleys, towers over the mountains in the environment by 300m, and is the mountain with the farthest visibility in Norway. The main peak, Gaustatoppen, offers a view spanning 50,000km^2: From Skagerrak and the skerry coast, Tryvasshøgda, from which a TV tower extends, near Oslo, and the Norwegian / Swedish frontier 175km further south, the view stretches across the mountain areas of Nisserfjella, Fyresdalsheiene, Setesdalsheiene and Lifjell, as well as over Hardangervidda and beyond to the Hardanderjøkulen glacier, up to the peaks of Jotunheimen, almost 180km further north. The romantic poet Aasmund Olafsson Vinje even described the rounded quartzite ridge, which from the north-west takes on the shape of a cone, and from the east, a dome, as the most beautiful mountain in Norway. The gullies in the flanks of Gausta may be filled with snow well into the summer: The average temperature near the summit is 4.6°C in July, and in February -10.6°. The recommended route is the easiest ascent; however, it is traversed by approximately 15,000 people annually.

The starting point is the parking area at **Stavsrobua**. From here, the panoramic, red-T marked mountain path leads through the flank of the **Gaustaråen** ridge. Shortly after passing a cross which stands in memoriam on the spot where someone was killed in 1992, the path merges with the route coming up from Svineroi. From this point of convergence, we continue following the markers to the left (west), and a short distance later, the path leading up from the chain of lakes in Gausdalen on the western foot of Gausta merges with our route, which now leads steeply up to **Gaustahytta**. The stone »hut«, which is supplied via a tunnel built for military purposes originating in Lange-fonn, possesses a variety of tourist wares: postcards, souvenirs, summit diplomas, stamps, stuffed troll dolls, etc. Somewhat more difficult is the ascent, which leads along a scree-strewn ridge and provides many vistas, and may seem exposed. It guides us in a good quarter of an hour to the actual summit, the **Gaustatoppen** (1881m).

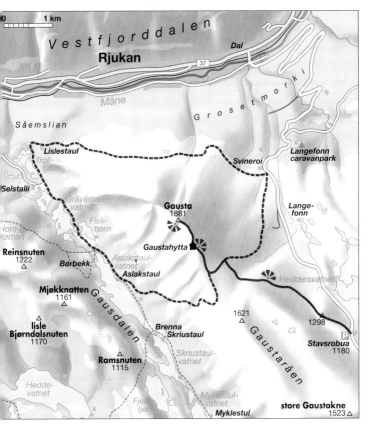

48 Blefjell-Hardangervidda Trail

Over the ridge of the Blefjell on the eastern edge of Hardangervidda

Nordstul – Sigridsbu – Eriksbu – Øvre Fjellstul – Daggrøhytta – Lufsjå – Imingfjell Turistheim

Location: The town of Kongsberg is situated in the southern Norwegian Fylke Buskerud on the lower reaches of the Fumesdalslågen River. Access via E 134 Oslo – Kongsberg – Haugesund.

Starting point: Car park (approx. 720m) in Blefjell at the end of the »Norstulveien« toll road south-east of Flesberg; head from Flesburg in the direction of Kongsberg, turn right onto Riksvei 37 in the direction of Rjukan; shortly after Bølkesjø, turn right in the direction of Store Blefjell.

Destination point: Imingfjell Turistheim; in this hostel, you can call a taxi for the return trip.

Walking times: Approx. 4–6 days, approx. 30 hrs. (approx. 80km).

Ascent: Moderate ascents of total approximately 2000m.

Grade: Sure-footedness, knowledge of weather.

Huts: Sigridsbu (1000m), KOT hut (18 berths, no provisions); Eriksbu (940m), KOT hut (20 berths, no provisions); Øvre Fjellstul (815m), DOT hut (10 berths, no provisions); Daggrøhytta (980m), DOT self-serviced hut (16 berths); Lufsjåhytta (1217m), TOT and DNT self-serviced hut (12 berths); Imingfjell Turistheim (1100m), private mountain hostel (34 berths).

Maps: Road map 1:325,000, Cappelens kart, p. 1 Sør-Norge sør; TK 50, p. 1614 I Tinnsjå, 1714 IV Flesberg, 1615 II Nore and 1615 III Tessungdalen.

The six legs of the Blefjell-Hardangervidda Trail between Nordstul in Blefjell and the Imingfjell hostel on the eastern edge of Hardangervidda lead through mountain terrain which has remained relatively isolated, and which, in its great diversity, introduces the hiker to just about all characteristics of the Norwegian fjell, and without the need of strenuous ascents and descents.

Gigantic panoramic views alternate with woody passages, and in between, idyllic mountain lakes invite you to rest and, in the right weather, go swimming. Now and then, you must wade through streams, then we are once again greeted by the beauty of the moorlands and expansive plateau-like hollows, and again and again, the sheer endless view of the mountain countryside in south-east Norway.

And on the sixth leg, we again traverse typical high-mountain terrain. In rainy weather, the boggy passages (especially on the third leg) can be wet, and, since the clear path is mostly, but not always, marked by a *red T*, you must always consult your maps at turnoffs without clear markers or signs.

Actually, the Blefjell-Hardangervidda Trail, one of the classic extended walks in southern Norway, begins in the town of Kongsberg in the lower Numedal; however, since the passage between Kongsberg and Blefjell follows National Road 37 for a while, it is more attractive to begin the walk in Blefjell.

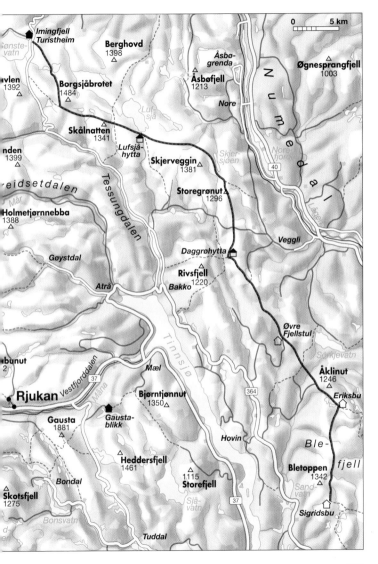

0   5 km

Imingfjell
Turistheim

Gønste-
vatn

Berghovd
1398

Åsbø-
grenda

Øgnesprangfjell
1003

vlen
1392

Borgsjåbrotet
1484

Åsbøfjell
1213

Nore

Luf-
sjå

N
u
m
e
d
a
l

Skålnatten
1341

Lufsjå-
hytta

Skjerveggin
1381

Skjer-
sjøen

nden
1399

eidsetdalen

Tessungdalen

Storegrønut
1296

Nore-
fjorden

40

Holmetjørnnebba
1388

Gøystdal

Daggrøhytta

Veggli

Atrå

Rivsfjell
1220

Bakko

Øvre
Fjellstul

Sørkjevatn

bunut
2

Mæl

Tinnsjø

Åklinut
1246

Rjukan

Vestfjorddalen

37

Måna

Bjørntjønnut
1350

364

Eriksbu

Gausta
1881

Gausta-
blikk

Hovin

Ble-

fjell

Heddersfjell
1461

1115
Storefjell

Bletoppen
1342

Skotsfjell
1275

Bondal

Sjå-
vatn

37

Sand-
vatn

Sigridsbu

Bonsvatn

d

Tuddal

In a virtually endless expanse of rock, water and green (we climb up Bletoppen), whereas the Blefjell-Hardangervidda Trail continues straight on.

1st Leg: Nordstul – Sigridsbu (6km, 2 hrs., approx. 500m. alt. ascent; TK 50, p. 1614 I Tinnsjå): This leg is identical to walk 44; see that description.

2nd Leg: Sigridsbu – Eriksbu (11km, 4 hrs., hardly any ascents; TK 50, p. 1614 I Tinnsjå): From the Sigridsbu hut, the *red-T* marked path leads further to the foot of Bletoppen (side-trip to summit, see walk 44), then through panoramic, flat, mountainous highlands to the Eriskbu hut on the Åklitjørnan chain of lakes.

3rd Leg: Eriksbu – Øvre Fjellstul (10km, 4 hrs., hardly any ascents; TK 50, p. 1614 I Tinnsjå): From the Eriksbu hut, the *T*-marked route leads through partially boggy highlands to the Øvre Fjellstul hut, which is situated in the forest.

4th Leg: Øvre Fjellstul – Daggrøhytta (13km, 4 hrs., hardly any ascents, TK 50, p. 1614 I Tinnsjå and 1615 II Nore): With the exception of a few panoramic high ridges, the *red-T* markers primarily lead through forest and moorland to the Daggrøhytta hut, which is situated on a small lake.

5th Leg: Daggrøhytta – Lufsjå (21km, 6–8 hrs., ascents approx. 500m. alt., TK 50, p. 1615 II Nore and 1615 III Tessungdalen): This leg, marked not with the *red T*, but rather, cairns, leads from the Daggrøhytta northwards, where, after crossing a side-street, the panoramic high-elevation walk begins. It soon follows the old *Nordmannsslepa* traffic route on Hardangervidda to the Lufsjå hut on the lake of the same name.

6th Leg: Lufsjå – Imingfjell Turistheim (17km, 6–8 hrs., few ascents; TK 50, p. 1615 III Tessungdalen): During the panoramic final leg (with a view to Gaustatoppen), the *Store Nordmannsslepa*, marked with stone markers, leads westward, until the *red T* marked path to the Imingfjell hut branches off to the north shortly before Borgsjå lake.

The hiking trails are marked with the red T (T stands for tur = walk) and stone markers.

49 Straight across Jotunheimen

Crossing the Jotunheimen Mountains from hut to hut

Hjelle – Skogadalsbøen – Leirvassbu – Gjendebu – Memurubu – Gjendesheim

Location: The community of Årdal is situated in the western Norwegian Fylke Sogn og Fjordane, and encompasses the south of the Hurrungane, the south-west of Jotunheimen and other mountain areas at the Årdalsfjord, foothills of the Sognefjord.

Starting point: Car park Hjelle (100m) in Utladalen; Access via E 16 Oslo – Fagernes – Tyinkrysset; there, turn off onto Riksvei 53 toward Øvre Årdal and turn right into Utladalen.

Destination point: Gjendesheim, bus stop

there on the Otta – Fagerness line; there, change to the bus in the direction of Øvre Årdal – Gol.

Walking times: Approx. 20 hrs. to Gjendebu (56km) with a continuation on a ship.

Ascent: Partially steep ascents of approx. 2300m. alt.

Grade: Sure-footedness, good physical condition.

Huts: Vetti Gård (680m), farm at Vettisfossen (opportunity to stop; overnight stay only upon previous reservation); Vettismorki

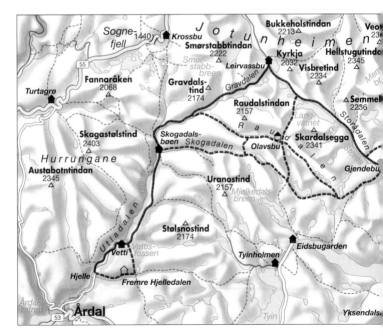

Descent to the Høgvagltjørnene lakes.

(683m), DNT hut owned by Vetti Gård (4 berths, no provisions); Vormeli (612m), an unstaffed stone hut without bedding in Utdalen which is not on the way, but accessible via a side-trip; Skogadalsbøen (843m), staffed DNT hut (55 beds) without public automobile access; Leirvassbu (1400m), mountain hotel (140 beds) with automobile access; Olavsbu (1440m, alternative route), DNT self-serviced hut (40 berths); Gjendebu (990m), staffed DNT hostel (115 berths); Memurubu (1008m), mountain hotel (140 beds); Gjendesheim (995m), DNT mountain hotel (143 beds).

Maps: TurK 100, p. Jotunheimen; TK 50, p. 1517 IV Hurrungane (only 2mm^2 of p. 1518 III Sygnefjell are needed) 1518 II Galdhøpiggen, 1517 I Tyin and 1617 IV Gjende.

This crossing of the Jotunheimen mountains, which is set up as a valley walk, leads from the Utladalen, through which waterfalls rush, and in which our starting point lies only a small amount above sea level, from hut to hut up to the Leirvassbu

View through Leirungsdalen across Gjende lake and beyond to the Surtningssui summit and – on the right – the dome of the Besshøi.

mountain hotel on the Kyrkja summit, and down to the Gjendebu hostel on Gjende lake.

Here, you have a choice: Either continue by ship or on foot (walking times see walk 30 and 29) to the final destination of Gjendesheim. Since the network of *red T* marked main hiking trails and secondary trails which are unmarked or occasionally marked with stone markers is relatively dense, the route allows ample room for alternative routes and side-trips.

1st Leg: Hjelle – Vettisfossen – Skogadalsbøen (6 hrs., 17km, ascents 1200m. alt., TK 50, p. 1517 IV Hurrungane): From Hjelle, this unpaved road closed to public traffic leads upward through the narrow, steep-walled, plant-rich Utladalen past several waterfalls, and up to the Vetti Gård farm. We continue on a path to Vettisfossen, which, with a 275-metre drop, is considered the largest waterfall in Norway. After passing the Vettismorki hut, the *red T* marked path, with its unique Hurrungane panorama, leads to the DNT hostel Skogadalsbøen.

2nd Leg: Skogadalsbøen – Gravdalen – Leirvassbu (6–8 hrs., 19km, ascents 700m. alt., TK 50, p. 1517 IV Hurrungane and 1518 II Galdhøpingen): From the DNT hostel Skogadalsbøen, the *red T* marked path leads along the slope further up the Utladalen and then swerves to the right, up in the

148

Storutledalen. There, on the border between the Utladalen conservation area and Jotunheimen National Park, lies a reservoir of Gravalsdammen. The most comfortable route in this grand high-mountain terrain is to start at the lake and walk up along the private factory road in Gravdalen, which is covered by patches of snow far into the summer (the *T* path leads mostly parallel to it). The end point of this leg, the Leirvassbu mountain hotel (see walk 28) lies in dazzling mountain/glacier scenery.

3rd Leg: Leirvassbu – Storådalen – Gjendebu (8 hrs., 20km, approx. 400m. alt., TK 50, p. 1518 II Galdhøpiggen, 1517 I Tyin and 1617 IV Gjende): From the Leirvassbu mountain hotel, we go back along the same route for a short time and then turn left in the direction of Gjendebu / Olavsbu (recommended alternative route). After crossing the pass at Kyrkja, the mountain path, marked with the *red T*, descending to Høgvagltjørnene lakes begins. After passing the Olavsbu turnoff, we walk along the Langvatnet and then downward through Storådalen to the Gjendebu hostel on the western bay of Gjende lake (ships' landing, no road access).

4th Leg: Gjendebu – Memurubu: see walk 30.

5th Leg: Memurubu – Gjendesheim: see walk 29.

A rest on Besseggen overlooking Gjende lake and Bessvatnet.

50 Lillehammer-Rondane Trail

From hut to hut, from Lillehammer to the Rondane mountains

Nordseter – Neverfjell – Pellestova – Djupsliseter – Vetåbua – Breitjønnbu – Gråhøgdbu – Eldåbu – Rondvassbu (Bjørnhollia)

Location: The town of Lillehammer is located in the eastern Norwegian Fylke Oppland where the Gudbrandsdalen flows into a widened area of Mjøsa lake. Olympia-Park (Lillehammer was the site of the 1994 Winter Olympics); Outdoor Museum Maihaugen. Access via E 6 Oslo – Lillehammer.

Starting point: Car park in the winter sport centre of Lillehammer-Nordseter (980m), accessible by bus from Lillehammer (railway station).

Destination point: Holiday town and winter sport centre of Mysuseter; from there, you can get the bus to the Otta railway station in Gudbrandsdalen, where there are direct railway connections to Lillehammer / Oslo.

Walking times: Approx. 35–40 hrs.; 121km

with the goal of reaching Mysuseter directly, 134km to Mysuseter via Rondvassbu.

Ascent: Moderate ascents of total time approx. 2000m.

Grade: Sure-footedness, good physical condition.

Huts: Pellestova (980m), mountain hotel; Djupsliseter (750m), LOT self-serviced hut (12 berths); Vetåbua (926m), LOT self-serviced hut (12 berths); Breitjønnbu (1160m), DNT self-serviced hut (8 berths); Gråhøgdbu (1160m), DNT self-serviced hut (8 berths); Eldåbu (1000m), DNT self-serviced hut (18 berths).

Maps: TK 50, p. 1817 II Lillehammer, 1817 I Goppollen, 1818 II Imsdalen and TurK 100 p. Rondane.

Norwegian raspberry.

Autumn colours: blueberry and birch.

The approximately 100-km long Lillehammer-Rondane Trail leads from hut to hut, without major ascents and descents at an average elevation of almost 1000m, from the winter sport centre Nordseter near the Olympian town of Lillehammer via Øyerfjellet, Fåvangfjellet, and Ringebufjellet in Rondane National Park.

This beautiful multi-leg walk (on skis, too) leads mainly above the tree line through panoramic terrain with lichen, lakes, woods, moorlands, mosses and meadows in which sheep graze. Only a few sections lead through wood, and streams must occasionally be waded across. The *red T* marked path crosses and/or touches on mountain-pasture paths, so a descent into the valley is possible. The national topographical maps are, to some extent, obsolete, but thanks to the markers, you can still find your way.

1st Leg: Nordseter – Neverfjell – Pellestova (2 hrs., 7km, 300m. alt. TK 50, p. 1817 II Lillehammer): The very start of this walk is a beautiful stretch. The *T*-marked path leads gently upward through woods, panoramic meadowland, and small bogs to the panoramic top of the Neverfjell (1089m), from where you have an overview of the entire route, right up to the Rondane Mountains; east of the Neverfjell, the view spans the Reinsvatnet and several other small lakes which, despite boggy spots, several hikers find a place to pitch a tent, and a few bays are also used for bathing.

If you have your tent along, you will generally find excellent camping spots again and again along the entire route – spots which, as the journey progres-

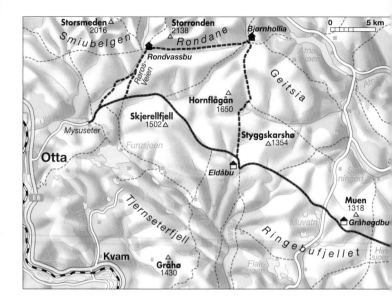

ses become isolated, whereas the Olympia area around Neverfjell and Pellestova are well-frequented.

From Neverfjell, the *T* markers guide us down to the Pellestova mountain hotel at the foot of the Hafjell (winter sport centre).

2nd Leg: Pellestova – Djupsliseter (6–8 hrs., 22km, TK 50, p. 1817 II Lillehammer and 1817 I Goppollen): From Pellestova on the south-western foot of the Hafjell, which is decorated with a ski-jumping hill, the Lillehammer-Rondane Trail follows a toll road for a long while roughly to the north-east between moorlands and the panoramic Reinsfjell. Soon after the intersection with the toll-road pass Gudbrandsdalen – Glåmatal, our road ends at the Sjøsæter mountain pasture; the *T*-marked path crosses the panoramic Sjøsæterfjellet (1048m) and leads through partially boggy terrain to the DNT hut Djupsliseter on the small Djupen reservoir.

3rd Leg: Djupsliseter – Vetåbua (5 hrs., 16km, TK 50, p. 1817 I Goppollen and 1818 II Imsdalen): From Djusplisseter, the trail leads over the panoramic Åstkyrkja, then through mountain pasture area, and later through moorlands, before reaching the Vetåbua hut on the Vetå River.

4th Leg: Vetåbua – Breitjønnbu (4 hrs, 14km, TK 50, p. 1818 II Imsdalen): The trail leads northward along the Breidjordan moorlands, crosses the twin domes of Gråhøgda, and reaches the Breitjønnbu hut.

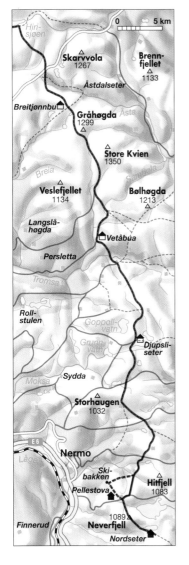

5th Leg: Breitjønnbu – Gråhøgdbu (6–8 hrs., 23km, TK 50, p. 1818 II Imsdalen and 1818 III Ringebu): The trail crosses the pass from Ringebu to Atna, at the huts on Hisrisjøen lake, switches to the right (north) to the old »Priests' Way«, then a short time later leaves this path to head west, and reaches the Gråhøgdbu hut, with a beautiful view of Muen.

6th Leg: Gråhøgdbu – Eldåbu (5 hrs., 17km, TK 50, p. 1818 III Ringebu and TurK 100, p. Rondane; the Eldåbu hut is only shown correctly on the latter map): From the Gråhøgdbu hut, the path takes us, along with a fine panorama, past the foot of Muen (walk 39) and merges onto Riksvei 27. We follow this road for a short time, and turn left on the road leading to the private Ramshytta.

There, the trail to the Eldåbu hut begins. Once there, you must decide whether to continue in the direction of Rondvassbu (6–8 hrs., see walk 34–36), or in the direction of Bjørnhollia (5–7 hrs., see walk 35) further into the Rondane Mountains.

7th Leg: Alternative route Eldåbu – Rondvassbu (6 hrs., 24km, TurK 100 Rondane, TK 50, p. 1718 I Rondane): From the Eldåbu hut, we follow the *T*-marked path back for a short distance, then turn left onto the signposted and *T*-marked path in the direction of Bjørnhollia. Shortly thereafter, this path crosses the border of the Rondane National Park, indicated by a stone marker, and right afterwards, reaches an intersection. Here, we turn left and walk to the north-west, in the directi-

From the Neverfjell near Lillehammer, one has an overview of the entire route, right up to the peaks of the Rondane Mountains.

on of »Rondvassbu / Mysuseter«. After crossing the Djupbekken stream, a tributary of the River Eldåa, we follow the latter upwards in the northern bank area, until, after 2½km, we come to two paths leading in from the right which lead to the river.

Here, we cross the river and follow it upward along its south-west bank, and after traversing a few bogs in which headstreams of the Eldåi collect, reach the panoramic col (1270m) between Skjerelfjellet and Steinbudalshøa. In the vicinity of this col, we find a few of the reindeer trap pits so typical of the Rondane area. With a splendid view of the highest Rondane mountains, the trail leads gently downward, and at P 1198 merges onto the path between Mysuseter (left) and Bjørnhollia (right). At this point, we continue to the left, following the headstream of the River Glitra downward. Soon after crossing the stream, we come to yet another crossroads.

Here, you can decide for one last time whether to continue on to Rondvassbu (2 more hours, 7 km, very pretty and panoramic stretch which merges with the transport road shortly before Rondvassbu) or go straight in the direction of Mysuseter.

7th Leg: Alternative route Eldåbu – Mysuseter, direct (6 hrs., 22km, TurK 100 Rondane, TK 50, p. 1718 I Rondane): If you continue straight ahead on the intersection last cited on an equally very panoramic route, you will come to the Mysuseter – Sprangent toll road around the first houses of Mysuseter after 1 hr. Follow the toll road down to the left into the holiday hut and winter sport village of Mysuseter. In Mysuseter, there are bus connections to the railway station in Otta.

8th Leg: Rondvassbu – Mysuseter (3 hrs., 11km, TurK 100 Rondane, TK 50, p. 1718 I Rondane): If you walked to the DNT mountain hotel Rondvassbu on the 7th leg, you still have the stretch from Rondvassbu – Mysuseter before you as the 8th leg. In principle, you can follow the transport road from Rondvassbu to the Sprangent car park, and then continue on the toll road to Mysuseter (total time 11km). This is a very panoramic stretch, but a road-intensive one, added to which is the fact that, from the Sprangent car park, it is not car-free.

An alternative to this is the Rørosveien, a historical trade route, which today is a panoramic trail: 2½km after Rondvassbu, it branches off of the transport road (before the transport road begins sloping downward), and leads, with an unequalled view, roughly to the south, where, after 4 km, it meets the path (on the left) leading past the Eldå hut. Here, we turn off to the right and walk down to Mysuseter; now in the winter sport and holiday village, the last bit follows the Mysuseter – Sprangent toll road.

At our destination in Bjørnhollia, we find in Skjerdalen (Villmanndalen) an enjoyable excursion site directly south of the hostel.

Index